REAL ESTATE
INVESTING
made
SIMPLE

REAL ESTATE
INVESTING
made
SIMPLE

YOUR GUIDE TO **BUILDING AND GROWING WEALTH**

ERIC ANDERSON
NOELLE FRIESON FRIEDMAN

WILEY

Published by John Wiley & Sons, Inc., Hoboken, New Jersey.
Published simultaneously in Canada.

For general information on our other products and services or for technical support, please contact our Customer Care Department within the United States at (800) 762-2974, outside the United States at (317) 572-3993 or fax (317) 572-4002.

Wiley also publishes its books in a variety of electronic formats. Some content that appears in print may not be available in electronic formats. For more information about Wiley products, visit our web site at www.wiley.com.

Library of Congress Cataloging-in-Publication Data is Available:

ISBN 9781394248322 (Paperback)
ISBN 9781394248339 (epub)
ISBN 9781394248353 (epdf)

Cover Design: Wiley
Cover Images: © Ismagilov/Getty Images, © BsWei/Getty Images

SKY10076372_060424

Contents

Introduction

We're honored to be here and share our exciting, sometimes scary, but always motivating stories about real estate investing!

We are passionate about real estate and the process that it takes to buy it, sell it, and hold it. We also think that if you've found our book, you must share that passion as well. It's also important for us to help people understand that real estate provides a solid path to acquire wealth that can change your life and the lives of your family for generations to come. We consider ourselves lucky that we found it—financial freedom through real estate! And in the pages ahead, we show you how you can find your own freedom through real estate, too.

Use our stories as a guide to help you navigate your own path whether you want to get the best deal on your next property, be a resource for your family and friends, or to become a real estate tycoon. Our book will teach you the successful approach we use at the Center for Real Estate Education, our real estate school, and our brokerage, Alexander Anderson Real Estate Group. Through the school we have given thousands of students the tools they need to be successful real estate entrepreneurs. Through our brokerage we have nurtured hundreds of agents and helped them to close deals with creative solutions to real estate opportunities and sometimes real estate problems.

Throughout this book, we offer guidance on how to think about the kinds of real estate you want to pursue and how to avoid common mistakes that can slow your progress. We help you to think about your strengths and play to them, while seeking help in the areas where you need it. Our goal is to take you—no matter your age or professional level—and put you on your journey into real estate investing by giving you a strong foundation and specific actions you can take to begin and thrive in this industry.

Good luck and never stop thinking about real estate!

Chapter 1

Why Real Estate Is a Great Way to Build Wealth

Real estate is one of the most time-tested and effective ways to acquire and maintain wealth. Unlike the value of stocks, which are keenly sensitive to the ebbs and flows of the market, real estate values have shown they exhibit a more stable investment proposition. Through our real estate school, The Center for Real Estate Education, more than 15,000 people have acquired the tools to chart their own path to wealth through real estate investing.

Why You Need a Wealth Plan

Everyone needs to develop a wealth plan. Without one there is no clear path to achieving financial success for you or your family. When we talk about a *wealth plan*, we're talking about a guide to attaining your financial freedom—one you can revisit and revamp as you proceed along your journey. These plans encompass multiple layers, including choosing the type of real estate you want to pursue, setting both short- and long-term goals, and evaluating tangible and intangible assets.

It's not merely about crunching numbers, though your current finances are a critical component. A wealth plan serves as the blueprint for your financial aspirations—a road map guiding you toward achieving them through real estate investing. As you develop a wealth plan, you'll examine your financial situation, needs, and the path to realizing your goals.

We understand that the day-to-day demands of life are constantly competing for your time and attention. Our most productive hours are consumed by family, work, and personal commitments. Starting today, carve out time to develop a wealth plan. Without one it will be difficult to develop financial independence, security, and peace of mind. A well-thought-out plan involves more than accumulating assets; it's composed of specific, measurable, and achievable financial goals while navigating through the constantly shifting market dynamics of the times.

When thinking about your wealth plan, you need to consider what type of cash flow you need to maintain your current lifestyle and the cash flow you will need to create the lifestyle you envision. This is the time to assess the steps, people, and resources you have and need to make your dreams a reality. A wealth plan will serve as a guide to help you break down your needs and tasks to set and achieve financial goals. It will also serve as a barometer to let you know if you are reaching your goals and getting closer to your objectives.

Well-thought-out plans consider potential risks to your financial health and provide strategies to lessen their impact. Risks are determined by your age and the number of financial responsibilities you have. The younger you are, the more time you have to recoup any failures; the older you are, the more likely you'll need direct access to your cash. This means using your wealth plan to note what the risks are and creating contingencies as a crucial part of your planning strategy.

This is why we can't overstate the importance of starting an emergency fund. There are always competing interests pulling cash away from your wallet, but you will never regret starting an emergency fund. Begin with a modest amount, such as $40 to $50 each pay period, and in time it will build up.

This is also the time to evaluate the kinds of insurance you may want to add to your portfolio. Different types of insurance policies, such as life, health, and property insurance, can provide financial security by covering surprise losses or expenses. Acquiring the right policies now will prevent unforeseen events from derailing your financial goals.

Why Real Estate Should Be Part of Your Wealth Plan

Real estate should be a central part of a wealth plan due to its potential for escalation in value, rental income, and tax benefits. Houses, office buildings, and parking lots are examples of tangible assets that offer a sense of security and control. Additionally, because you can literally kick the foundation to check its condition, you have more control over your investment.

An additional benefit to investing in and acquiring real estate is that it creates the opportunity to build generational wealth for your family. *Generational wealth* refers to assets that are passed down from one generation to the next. As for real estate, once you own it, the property can last for generations and continue to provide passive income.

For instance, a family could decide to acquire a two-family home and use the top-floor apartment as a rental property to service the mortgage. Once there's a positive cash flow, the additional income could help to fund several priorities such as saving for more properties, retirement, college tuition, or debt resolution.

We have witnessed the financial flexibility that real estate offers. Let's say you become a real estate flipper. In this role, you might notice an old house or building that's boarded up and for sale, and decide to buy it and renovate it. If you don't want to wear a hard hat and goggles, you could just invest money, hire contractors, and not put any hard labor or "sweat equity" into the project.

There are many paths to wealth building within real estate. Take the time to figure out the type of real estate you want to leverage to achieve your financial goals. To ensure that you're on track, create a list of core action items with achievable deadlines to help you stay focused. Having a plan ensures that you have structure and helps you achieve a goal. If you just went in without a plan, you might feel as if you are winning the battle, but you might not win the financial freedom war.

Part of this process is figuring out how you want to define success. Is it a couple of bucks of additional income to pad your retirement? Or do you want to get enough passive income so you don't have to do whatever you're doing now? We think that's probably what success looks like to most people.

Case Study: Here's What Can Happen When a Wealth Plan Is a Priority

We had a student named Sarah who joined Alexander Anderson Real Estate Group. She was a college student and knew that she wanted to go into real estate; however, after attending the Center for Real Estate Education and taking some of the investment classes on top of her mandatory pre-licensing course, she set her sights on a career in real estate investment. The most important lesson she took from the investment classes was that to make her dream a reality, she needed a solid plan—a wealth plan that she could revisit from time to time, revamp, and fall back on when she felt that she was gearing off course.

While getting her real estate license, Sarah meticulously put together her wealth plan. She diligently researched the local market in which she wanted to work, studied investment strategies, and always sought advice from instructors and other seasoned professionals. Throughout her studies, Sarah absorbed every piece of information like a sponge. The pre-licensing course provided her with a strong foundation of the legalities within real estate. But the extra investment courses really opened her eyes to what more could be done within the real estate industry, specifically, buying and holding real estate.

On obtaining her real estate license, Sarah dove headfirst into the industry. She worked in both commercial and residential real estate to start. She worked with mentors in both divisions of Alexander Anderson Real Estate Group, getting to know the differences between working with people seeking the perfect home and business-minded professionals looking for space that would fit their bottom-line numbers.

Sarah excelled at networking. She loved talking to people, but even more she loved listening to people, learning their stories, and figuring out how she could help them even if at that very

(continued)

(continued)

moment they could not help her. For over a year, she networked tirelessly, attending seminars and workshops, and connecting with potential clients. Her knowledge and passion for the market were evident, and soon, she started closing deals.

She gravitated to commercial real estate, learning quickly that as she listened to various entrepreneurs and professionals she not only could help them find the perfect office space or retail space but also she could help them find a location that would fit their business models as well. As the commissions began to flow in and Sarah saved money, Sarah got an opportunity, through contacts she had gained, to invest in a building in an up-and-coming area of a New Jersey. It was a big investment for such a young and new professional. But because she knew that it fit into her wealth plan—which also took into consideration that she was in her twenties with very few responsibilities—she decided to take the plunge. She invested $30,000 into the building with several other partners. Though it wasn't as much as some of the partners were investing, it gave her an opportunity to start her portfolio. Sarah received monthly distributions from this property, and though it wasn't enough for her to retire, she recognized the potential for growth. Sarah expanded her horizons.

It's been three years and Sarah now has a small but solid portfolio of real estate investments. She is now looking to flip individual single-family homes with some of the construction contacts she has made over the years. She's still working in commercial real estate sales, but she is well on her way to financial freedom, using her earnings as an agent to build her real estate portfolio.

She would have never taken her first investment opportunity seriously if it had not been for her wealth plan. It was in writing—it reminded her that even though the opportunity was scary and a big leap for her, it was what she had envisioned for herself before she even became a real estate agent.

How to Get Your Head in the Real Estate Game

Knowledge is power. Read as many books as you can and start reading about what it's like to own and manage real estate. Your book list must include a glossary of real estate terms. In the real estate industry, you will hear words that you have never heard before. Becoming familiar with real estate terms helps you identify opportunities when you hear them.

Focus on the content that interests you most—residential, commercial, house flipping, value-add investments, or sales. If you are inspired after soaking up all this knowledge, and you want to begin a career in real estate, then consider taking steps to get your license.

Get a Real Estate License

Getting a real estate license isn't a must if you want to be a real estate investor, but it's a smart move for a few good reasons. First off, the process of acquiring a license will give you a greater understanding of how the real estate sector operates. You will become well versed on the rules, the laws, and how the market works. This knowledge gives you the power to make smart choices, analyze deals, and handle tricky situations with confidence. Having a license will give you an edge over other investors. You'll be privy to insider information and first opportunities to see properties that non-licensed investors won't have access to.

Plus, having a license lets you join a bigger group of real estate professionals—like agents, brokers, and experts. This group can be helpful in finding good investment opportunities, getting advice, and teaming up for successful deals. Last, if you are a licensed agent, you can handle your own transactions. This means you don't have to pay a big chunk of your profits in commissions. It gives you more freedom and control over your investments, which can lead to making more money in the long run. So, although it's not a must-do, getting a real estate license is a smart move if you want to be a successful real estate investor.

Find Like-Minded People

Whether you get your real estate license or not, it is also important to network. Go out there and find people who are doing what you want to do. Find people who are investing in real estate and talking about real estate. There are numerous social media groups or networking groups that you can join to immerse yourself in the language and culture of buying and selling property. Find someone and offer to buy them a cup of coffee; ask to hang out with them for a day to see how they operate when buying or selling. Also, don't limit yourself to one person.

Go out there and find multiple people to network with who are doing different types of real estate and find people in different age groups. Seek out seasoned real estate professionals, people who have been doing this their whole life. They are going to give you amazing insight on what it is like to own real estate. They can tell you how to navigate in good and bad market conditions, and what to look out for. But don't stop there. Also, reach out to younger professionals who have 5 or 10 years of experience to discover what you can learn. Perhaps they have been effective with using social media to acquire and sell properties or using alerts when new properties become available in your market.

Cast a Wide Net

When you are in the early stages of your real estate path, cast a wide net and gather all the information you can about the city or town and the neighborhoods you plan to do business in. Pay attention to real estate articles in your local paper and community websites that feature property listings. Remember, these steps are only the beginning of how you can get up to speed on what's happening in your market. It's a good practice to read all you can and consume a healthy dose of YouTube instructional videos. Most likely you won't hit your stride until you develop a network of people that includes real estate agents, contractors, and financial professionals.

Also, as a novice player in the real estate market, it is best to focus on one property type until you have developed a high level of competency in either residential or commercial properties. Each category has its own risks and rewards. But no matter what area you choose—you can't sit on the sidelines forever. You've got to jump in and start. As the saying goes, "you've gotta be in it to win it."

So Many Choices: Start with One Property Type

Real estate investment offers a wide array of property types to choose from—commercial, multifamily, single-family, warehouses, and even land. It can be overwhelming, and you might be tempted to dive into multiple types at once. However, for new investors, here's the scoop: it's a smart move to start with just one property type. This approach will help you gradually navigate the world of real estate investing and find your comfort zone. Let's explore a variety of property types and the potential risks and rewards associated with each.

Top Five Rewards of Investing Mid-Size to Large Commercial Properties

1. **Bigger payouts.** Due to the higher value of these buildings brokers and agents routinely get larger commissions as a real estate agent and larger payouts as an investor compared to smaller commercial properties or residential sales.

2. **Longer leases.** When you're buying and holding commercial property, occupants in commercial properties typically have longer term leases that provide steady income for the new owner.

3. **Diversification.** For investors, creating a mix of mid-size to large commercial properties in their portfolio can foster diversification and reduce the risk linked to a particular type of property.

4. **Advantage of size.** Owning larger properties often allows for economies of scale for services like maintenance, security, and management.

5. **Potential for appreciation.** Due to their prominence and potential for redevelopment or repositioning, large commercial properties might have higher appreciation potential, especially in growing markets.

Top Five Risks of Investing in Mid-Size to Large Commercial Properties

1. **Higher seed capital.** Large commercial properties usually require a substantial capital commitment compared to smaller properties or residential investments.

2. **Sophisticated management team.** Larger properties might require a complex management team, including more staff, rigorous maintenance schedules, and specialized systems.

3. **Greater risk exposure.** If a prominent tenant moves, it can lead to substantial income loss until a comparable replacement is found.

4. **Liquidity issues.** It is often harder to execute a quick sale of a large commercial property because they have a smaller pool of buyers, which incurs a prolonged sale process.

5. **High maintenance costs.** Larger buildings with a significant amount of people generally mean greater wear and tear and likely higher repair bills.

Top Five Rewards of Investing in Single-Family Homes

1. **High demand.** For decades single-family homes have been in steady demand among buyers. They are part of the fabric of the American Dream.

2. **Easy to finance.** In addition to conventional financing, there are plenty of assistance programs that can be accessed by the

general public and specific groups such as first-time home buyers, veterans, teachers, nurses, and members of police and fire departments.

3. **Quicker sales process.** There is a swift sales process for single-family homes, which is usually faster than larger commercial properties or multiunit residences.

4. **Large audience.** Single-family homes attract a wide range of buyers that include first-time homebuyers, downsizers, and investors.

5. **It's the American Dream.** Buyers often have an emotional attachment to buying their first home. This can often lead to a faster than usual sale process where cost takes a backseat to desire.

Top Five Risks of Investing in Single-Family Homes

1. **Unstable market.** Volatility in the real estate market can spur a decrease in home prices that, if you choose to sell in a down market, could lead to a loss for sellers who purchased their dwelling at a higher price.

2. **High transaction costs.** When flipping a single-family home, you will incur several transaction costs, which include agent commissions, closing costs, staging expenses, and, if needed, repair and renovation costs to increase the property's marketability or have the sale go through.

3. **Liquidity issues.** Houses, unlike stocks or bonds, are not suited for a quick sale. Depending on market conditions it can take weeks and sometimes months to find a buyer.

4. **Time-consuming.** Flipping a home doesn't always happen overnight. It can often feel more like a journey than a destination point. It must be prepped for sale, shown to potential buyers, then tested by inspectors. This phase can carry on for months if unexpected property conditions surface.

5. **Emotions can run high.** A family home is more than four walls and a roof. It is the keeper of our best memories and our most ambitious dreams. The personal attachment may make it difficult for the buyer or seller to acquire a new address.

In the chapters ahead, we'll guide you through the process of leveraging real estate investing to build wealth and achieve financial freedom. Yet, it's important to understand that it's not merely about amassing wealth. It involves introspection, identifying strengths and weaknesses, pinpointing your niche within real estate, and cultivating meaningful connections. Your wealth plan serves as the road map for this transformative journey.

Chapter 2

The Many Roads to Riches

Exploring the Diverse Avenues of Real Estate Investing

You've decided to dive into the world of real estate investing. Exciting, isn't it? But we get it—it can also feel a bit like standing at the foot of a mountain. There's so much to learn, and the paths to success are as varied as they are numerous. But, remember this— every seasoned investor started right where you are now. They too had to navigate through a sea of information and learn as they went along. One of the most important aspects of real estate investing is gaining a solid understanding of the different types of real estate and the ways you can invest in them.

Knowing all the ways you can invest in real estate lends to a diverse portfolio, which enables you, the investor, to take advantage of opportunities as they come around. You see, investing is a bit like a game of chess. It's all about strategy, and one of the best strategies is to not put all your eggs in one basket. Spreading your investments across different areas can help manage risk and increase your chances of seeing a return. When it comes to real estate, diversification could mean investing in different types of properties—think residential, commercial, or real estate investment trusts (REITs). Or it could mean investing in properties in different locations. Throughout this chapter, we take a look at each of these investment options. We talk about what they involve, how they work, and the potential risks and rewards. So, whether you're just starting out on your investment journey, or you're an old hand looking to diversify your portfolio, there's something here for you!

The Different Types of Real Estate

When people think about real estate investing, they often picture buying a house or an apartment and renting it out. And sure, that's one way to do it. But guess what? That's just the tip of the iceberg. There's a whole world of different types of real estate out there and different ways to invest, each with its own unique set of advantages and challenges.

- **Residential properties.** These are the homes we live in— houses, apartments, townhouses, you name it. We include vacation and short-term rentals in this category as well. Investing in residential properties is pretty straightforward. You buy a property, rent it out, or flip it for a profit and voila! You have a stream of income. But like every investment, it comes with its own set of challenges. You'll need to deal with tenants, maintenance issues, and market fluctuations. But if done right, it can be quite profitable.

- **Commercial properties.** These are office buildings, retail spaces, warehouses, and more. Commercial properties can be a bit more complex than residential ones. They often involve longer leases and can provide a more stable and substantial income. But they also require a bigger initial investment. Industrial real estate is often included in the commercial property category. These properties, which include everything from warehouses to factories, can offer high returns, but they come with their own unique challenges, such as zoning laws and environmental considerations.

- **Land properties.** Raw, undeveloped land can be a risky investment, but it can also be incredibly rewarding if you play your cards right.

- **Real estate investment trusts (REITs)** and **real estate crowdfunding.** Think of these as the mutual funds of the real estate world. They allow you to invest in real estate without having to buy a physical property.

Understanding the different types of real estate is just the first step. The real magic happens when you start to diversify your portfolio by investing in a mix of these options.

Rental Properties: The Classic Path to Real Estate Riches

Let's start with one of the most traditional and time-tested ways to invest in real estate: rental properties. There's something about owning a piece of land or a building and generating income from it that just feels right, doesn't it? But before you start picturing yourself as the next big real estate mogul, it's important to understand the nitty-gritty details.

Rental properties are pretty much what they sound like—properties that you buy with the intention of renting them out to tenants. The rent you collect becomes your income, and if all goes well, you'll earn more in rent than you spend on mortgage payments, maintenance, and other expenses. Simple, right? Well, in theory, yes. But as with all things, the devil is in the details.

Types of Rental Properties: Residential, Commercial, and Industrial

Rental properties come in all shapes and sizes:

- **Residential rental properties** are homes that people live in. Think houses, apartments, duplexes, and so on.
- **Commercial rental properties** include office buildings, retail spaces, restaurants, and other places where businesses operate.
- **Industrial rental properties** include warehouses, factories, and other types of industrial facilities.

Each type comes with its own set of challenges and rewards. Residential properties might be easier to understand for beginners, but commercial and industrial properties can offer higher returns and longer lease agreements.

Buying and Managing Rental Properties

Buying a rental property involves finding a suitable property, securing financing (unless you're lucky enough to be able to pay cash), closing the deal, and then finding tenants.

Managing the property can involve everything from collecting rent and handling maintenance issues to dealing with problem tenants and keeping the property occupied. It's not always a walk in the park, but don't fret; you can hire a property manager to handle most of these tasks for you, though that does eat into your profits.

Risks and Rewards of Owning Rental Properties

So, what are the risks and rewards of owning rental properties? One of the biggest benefits of investing in rental properties is the potential for steady cash flow. If you've ever dreamed of sitting back and watching the rent checks roll in every month, this could be your ticket. And who doesn't love the idea of earning money while they sleep?

Another major perk is the potential for property appreciation. While rental income can provide a steady stream of cash, the real jackpot often comes when you sell the property. If the property's value has gone up over time, you could be looking at a hefty profit.

But it's not all sunshine and rainbows. Owning rental properties can also be time-consuming and stressful, especially if you're doing all the management yourself. One of the biggest challenges is dealing with tenants. Finding good ones can be like finding a needle in a haystack, and even when you do, there's always the risk they might turn into a pumpkin at midnight (or, you know, stop paying rent or damage the property).

Another potential downside is the cost and hassle of property maintenance. Unlike stocks or bonds, properties require ongoing care and attention. Things break, wear out, or just plain go wrong. And guess who's on the hook for fixing them?

A major challenge is managing vacancies. A vacant unit is a financial drain, contributing no income while still incurring costs. The biggest cost is typically the mortgage payment that doesn't pause just because your property is unoccupied. If you depend on the rent you receive to cover your mortgage payment on the building, vacancies can swiftly turn into a financial liability, as you'll be responsible for covering the mortgage payment out of pocket. This scenario underlines the importance of effective property management, ensuring high occupancy rates, and maintaining an emergency fund to cushion against such eventualities.

Investing in rental properties can be a great way to generate income and build wealth over time. But like all investments, it's not without risks. The key is to do your homework, understand what you're getting into, and make informed decisions.

Case Study: Finding Success with the BRRRR Method

A topic that often pops up in our investment classes and gets everyone buzzing is the BRRRR method. No, we're not talking about the sound you make when you're freezing. *BRRRR* stands for *buy, rehab, rent, refinance, repeat*, and the BRRRR method is a hot real estate investment strategy that many savvy real estate investors are using to build their wealth quickly.

- **Buy.** The first step involves buying a distressed or underappreciated property below market value.

- **Rehab.** Next, this property is renovated and rehabilitated, increasing its value.

- **Rent.** Once the rehab is complete, the property is rented out to tenants, beginning the cash flow cycle.

- **Refinance.** The investor then refinances the property at its new, higher value, often recovering much or all of the initial investment.

- **Repeat.** Take the money from the refinance, and repeat the whole process again!

(continued)

(continued)

The brilliance of this method ties back to its cyclic nature, allowing for continuous rolling over of the initial investment into increasing property holdings.

A former student in our BRRRR course, Scott, felt stuck in a nine-to-five desk job. His ultimate inspiration (more on that in Chapter 4) was to have more freedom in his schedule and to be able to travel. When he joined the class, he was skeptical that he could achieve this goal through real estate, but Scott became one of our biggest converts. Scott's journey from office drone to successful real estate investor seems remarkable but it shows what hard work and perseverance can achieve.

Scott had a keen eye for undervalued properties; he enjoyed driving around various neighborhoods and finding properties that he felt in his gut had rehab potential. He bought his first property, a small multifamily property in Pennsylvania. Scott worked to rehab it, rented it out, refinanced his initial investment, and then he did it all over again.

With each cycle, Scott's rental portfolio grew, as did his monthly cash flow. The beauty of the BRRRR method is that it enabled him to leverage his initial investments, essentially using the same pot of money to accumulate more and more properties.

Fast-forward to just under two years later, and Scott's rental income had matched his day job salary. His hard work and strategic investing paid off, enabling him to quit his nine-to-five job and focus full-time on real estate.

In Scott's own words, "Investing using the BRRRR method isn't just about generating wealth; it's about creating the lifestyle you desire." And, boy, did he hit the nail on the head! Today, Scott enjoys the financial independence he had always dreamed of, all thanks to the power of the BRRRR method.

So, if you're sitting there, like Scott once was, yearning for a change and dreaming of financial freedom, take it from him: the BRRRR method could be your golden ticket. It's not just about the money; it's about crafting the life you've always wanted.

House Flipping: From Fixer-Upper to Fortune

Now let's explore the fast-paced world of house flipping. You've likely seen the HGTV shows: an investor buys a rundown house, fixes it up, sells it for a hefty profit, and repeats the process. Sounds like a dream, right? Well, it can be, but there's more to it than what you see on TV, much more.

What Is House Flipping?

House flipping is basically the process of buying a property with the intention of selling it quickly for a profit. The "flip" usually involves some level of renovation—anything from a fresh coat of paint to a full-on gut job. The idea is to increase the home's value so you can sell it for more than you invested, including the purchase price and renovation costs.

House flipping is a bit like baking a cake: you need the right ingredients and the right recipe. In this case, the ingredients are the property itself, the money to buy and renovate it, and the skills or resources to get the job done. And the recipe? Well, that's the process of finding, financing, fixing, and flipping.

Finding the Property

Finding the right property is key in both flipping and the BRRRR method described in the previous case study. Picture yourself as a treasure hunter, combing through the vast real estate market and looking for hidden gems. You're not on the hunt for just any old property; you need undervalued properties, maybe a little worse for wear, but brimming with untapped potential.

Maybe they've been neglected or fallen into disrepair. Perhaps they're outdated, stuck in a time warp from a bygone era. Or it could be they've got issues that have scared off other buyers—structural problems, a leaky roof, or a less-than-stellar location. But where others see problems, you see opportunity.

These are the homes that, with a bit of care, creativity, and elbow grease, can be transformed from ugly ducklings into beautiful swans.

It's not just about making them look pretty. It's about enhancing their value, making them desirable to renters or buyers, and turning a tidy profit in the process.

Finding these properties can be a challenge, sure. It involves research, patience, and sometimes thinking outside the box. But when you spot that diamond in the rough and envision what it could become, all that effort becomes worth it.

Financing the Property

Financing is when you get to play the game of Monopoly in real life! But instead of fake paper money, you're dealing with actual funds needed to buy and spruce up your property.

Financing can come from a variety of sources, and it's all about figuring out what works best for you. Maybe you've got a nice nest egg saved up that you're ready to invest—that's great! Your own cash can be a straightforward way to jump-start the process.

But maybe you're like many of us and don't have a hefty pile of cash lying around. No worries! That's where options like traditional mortgages come into play. You know, the kind you'd get from a bank or other financial institution.

Or perhaps you're looking at a fixer-upper that needs quite a bit of work—something most conventional lenders might shy away from. In that case, a hard money loan could be your ticket. These are short-term loans from private investors specifically designed for rehab projects like these. The real advantage of hard money loans is that they often place less emphasis on your personal credit score and more on the potential profitability of the investment deal you're interested in. And who says you have to stick to just one of these options? Sometimes, a combination of these financing methods might be the perfect recipe for your investment strategy.

So, whether you're self-financing, borrowing from a bank, seeking a hard money loan, or mixing and matching these options, remember: financing is all about securing the means to make your real estate dreams come true. It's not just about buying the property; it's about transforming it into a valuable asset that'll bring you returns in the long run.

Fixing the Property

Fixing is where the magic happens. The fixing phase is the next major step in house flipping. This is where you roll up your sleeves and transform that diamond in the rough into a sparkling gem.

Now, when we say "fixing," we're not just talking about slapping on a coat of paint and calling it a day. No, this is where you really get to flex your creative muscles and bring your vision to life. Maybe the kitchen needs a complete overhaul with new cabinets, countertops, and modern appliances. Or you want to transform the bathroom with new tiles, a stylish vanity, and updated fixtures.

Fixing is also about looking at the bigger picture and considering the overall layout and flow of the home. Sometimes, to achieve a better living space flow, you might need to restructure the layout of rooms. This could involve adding or knocking down walls to create a more open, airy, and functional space. For example, in the kitchen, you could consider removing a wall to create an open-plan living and dining area. This not only provides more space but also allows for better interaction and connectivity within the home. Perhaps you might create a dedicated workspace, or reading nook that might add value and functionality to the room.

And let's not forget the exterior—while a well-maintained lawn and appealing landscaping can certainly boost curb appeal, consider other elements too. Upgrading the front door area, for instance, can significantly add value to your home. When undertaking an investment renovation, remember it's not just about the individual elements, but how they all come together to create a harmonious, inviting, and functional living environment.

Although it's important to enhance the property's aesthetics, it's equally crucial to address any underlying issues. This could be anything from fixing leaky pipes and electrical faults to addressing structural problems and insulation issues.

When fixing up the property, it is also key to keep your target market in mind. Are you renovating for a family, young professionals, or maybe retirees? Each group will have different needs and wants, which should guide your renovation decisions.

So, yes, the fixing phase is most certainly where the magic happens. It's where you take a property that's seen better days and breathe new life into it, making it a home someone would love to live in. It's a challenging, sometimes exhausting process, but seeing the transformation and knowing you played a part in it—now, that's truly rewarding!

Flipping the Property

Flipping is the selling phase, the grand finale of the house-flipping process. This is when all your hard work, time, and investment come to fruition. You've done it! You've taken a worn-out property, rolled up your sleeves, and turned it into an absolute gem. You've overhauled the kitchen with modern appliances, revamped the bathroom with stylish fixtures, maybe even knocked down a wall or two to create a more open, inviting space. Your property isn't just "livable" now; it's a home someone would be proud to own.

Now comes the exciting part—it's time to put that beauty on the market! This is where you get to showcase all the improvements you've made, highlighting the features that make your property stand out. You've given this house a new lease on life, and now it's ready to bring joy to a new owner.

But remember, selling isn't just about listing the property and waiting for offers to roll in. It's about marketing it effectively, setting a competitive price, negotiating with potential buyers, and navigating through the closing process.

If you're not a real estate agent, you'll want to work with one who not only knows the local market inside and out but also understands the unique aspects of selling flipped properties. They can help you set a price that's enticing to buyers yet still gives you a nice profit margin. And hopefully, after all the viewings, negotiations, and paperwork, you'll sell your flipped house for a tidy sum, making all that hard work worth it. And then, you get to do it all over again with the next property!

In the end, the selling phase is not just about recouping your investment; it's the exciting climax of the house-flipping journey, when you see the fruits of your labor and, ideally, enjoy the financial rewards of a job well done.

Risks and Rewards of House Flipping

Now, let's talk about the risks and rewards of flipping houses. On the reward side, the potential profits can be substantial. If you buy low, renovate wisely, and sell high, you could make a tidy sum.

But house flipping is not without its risks. Renovations can uncover costly surprises (hello, unexpected plumbing issues!). The housing market could cool off, leaving you with a property you can't sell. And if you're not careful, renovation costs can spiral out of control, eating into your profits.

Case Study: From Infestation to Inspiration

Elaina, a former student, is now a seasoned house flipper. But when she first started out she found herself in an unexpected predicament. As a house flipper, Elaina had already taken on three challenging projects and turned them into profitable ventures. But her fourth project tested her skills and resilience like never before.

Elaina had recently purchased a quaint, mid-century home with plans to restore it to its former glory. The property had seen better days, but Elaina was undeterred. She saw past the outdated decor and overgrown yard, envisioning a charming home that any buyer would be lucky to own. However, there was one problem she hadn't anticipated: termites.

The termite infestation was far more extensive than she had initially thought. While the house sat on a concrete slab and the attic was damage-free, the pests had made themselves at home in the wooden structures of the property. This wasn't just a minor setback; it was a significant problem that threatened to skyrocket the costs of her flip.

(continued)

(continued)

But Elaina was determined not to let this hurdle derail her project. She immediately sought professional help to eradicate the pests. The home was treated, and she even secured a one-year warranty for the treatment. Despite this, the damage caused by the termites was considerable, and repairing it was costly.

Elaina knew that cutting corners wasn't an option. She had heard stories of unethical house flippers who failed to address such issues properly, only for them to resurface later for the new residents. She was committed to delivering quality homes and wouldn't compromise her reputation.

So, she rolled up her sleeves and got to work. It took additional time and investment, but eventually, she found the right company to repair the termite damage. The costs of the flip had indeed skyrocketed, but Elaina saw it as a learning experience.

When the house was finally ready and hit the market, Elaina was proud of her dedication and commitment. She had turned a termite-infested house into a beautiful, pest-free home. And when it sold, she found that her hard work paid off—not just in financial terms but also in the satisfaction of overcoming a significant challenge.

Elaina's story is a reminder that house flipping can come with unexpected obstacles. But with determination, ethical practices, and a commitment to quality, even the most daunting challenges can be overcome.

House flipping can be a rewarding and profitable venture, but it's not for the fainthearted. It requires time, money, and a good dose of courage. But if you're willing to roll up your sleeves and take on the challenge, it could be your ticket to real estate riches. But as with all investing, do your homework and go in with your eyes wide open.

Commercial Real Estate: Playing in the Big Leagues

Eric absolutely loves commercial real estate—he's like a kid in a candy store with it. He often tells folks who are new to investing, "You think residential real estate gets your heart racing? Just wait until you dip your toes into the commercial side of things. It's like going from little league to stepping up to bat in the World Series." But hey, if this makes you nervous, it's okay—we've got your back, and we'll guide you every step of the way.

What Is Commercial Real Estate?

Commercial real estate refers to properties designed for business use. Unlike residential real estate, which provides a place for people to live, commercial real estate provides spaces where businesses can thrive. There are several types of commercial real estate, including office, retail, industrial, multifamily, and mixed-use properties.

Office Properties

Office properties can be as diverse as the businesses that occupy them. On one end of the spectrum, you've got those iconic skyscrapers that define the skyline of downtown business districts—think Wall Street or Silicon Valley. These are the powerhouses of commerce, filled with bustling offices where big decisions are made. They're often home to large corporations, law firms, tech startups, and more. And let's not forget the amazing views these buildings usually offer.

Then, on the other end, there are small office buildings located in suburban areas. These might not have the glitz and glamour of their skyscraper counterparts, but they play a crucial role. They're typically home to local businesses, professional services like dentists and lawyers, or even regional branches of larger companies.

These buildings often offer a different vibe—a little quieter, a little more relaxed, but still buzzing with activity. Plus, they're conveniently located close to where people live, which can be a big plus for employees tired of long commutes.

So, whether it's a towering skyscraper or a modest two-story building in the 'burbs, office properties are a key part of the commercial real estate world. Each type has its own unique appeal and potential for investment.

Retail Properties

Retail properties are a fascinating part of the commercial real estate world. First, you've got your shopping malls. These are like the big leagues of retail properties. They're usually massive structures housing a mix of large department stores and smaller specialty shops. They are places where you can buy a new outfit, grab a bite to eat, watch the latest blockbuster, and even get a haircut, all under one roof.

Next up are strip malls. Now, these aren't as grand as shopping malls, but they've got their own charm. Your typical strip mall is a row of stores lined up side by side along a busy road. They usually house a mix of local businesses, from grocery stores and restaurants to services like dry cleaners and nail salons.

Stand-alone stores are individual retail buildings that house just one tenant. You'll often see big-box retailers like Walmart or Target in these types of properties, but they can also be home to smaller businesses. One of the biggest perks of stand-alone stores is their visibility—they're easy to spot, and they usually come with plenty of parking space.

Industrial Properties

Industrial properties might not be as glamorous as office towers or shopping malls, but they are incredibly important and have their own unique appeal.

First are warehouses. These are large buildings typically used for storing goods. You know when you order something online and it arrives at your doorstep a few days later? It's likely that the product was stored in a warehouse somewhere before it was shipped to you.

Next up, we have manufacturing plants. These are where goods are actually produced. Think of a factory where cars are assembled or a plant where your favorite snack foods are made. These facilities often require specific types of equipment and infrastructure, which makes them a specialized type of industrial property.

Then there are distribution centers. These are in the middle between warehouses and consumers. They're where goods are received, sorted, and then shipped out to their final destination. Because of the rise of e-commerce, these types of properties are becoming increasingly important.

So, although industrial properties might not be the first thing that comes to mind when you think of real estate investing, they play a crucial role in our everyday lives. They're the backbone of our economy, facilitating the production, storage, and distribution of goods. From an investment perspective, they can offer steady returns and long-term leases, which can attract those looking for a stable income stream.

Multifamily Properties

Now, you might be thinking, "Wait a minute, aren't those residential?" And you'd be right—to an extent. While multifamily properties do involve residences, when you start talking about larger ones like apartment complexes, the line between residential and commercial starts to blur. That's because these types of properties are often run more like a business than a traditional home.

Imagine for a moment you're the owner of a big apartment complex. You're not just responsible for one unit; you could oversee dozens, maybe even hundreds, of individual apartments. That means rent collection, maintenance, marketing vacant units, and so much more—all tasks that are more akin to running a business than managing a single-family home.

So, in the real estate world, these larger multifamily properties get lumped into the commercial category. They offer a unique investment opportunity, combining elements of both residential and commercial real estate. Plus, they can provide a steady stream of rental income, which is always a nice perk!

Multifamily properties are a fascinating hybrid in the real estate universe. They have the residential aspect because, well, people live there. But they're also commercial because they operate on a scale and with a more business-like complexity. It's a best-of-both-worlds scenario that makes them a favorite among many real estate investors.

Mixed-Use Properties

Mixed-use properties are a really interesting part of the real estate world. So, what are they exactly? Well, as the name suggests, these properties mix different types of uses all in one place—typically, they are a blend of residential, commercial, and sometimes even industrial spaces.

Imagine living in an apartment where you can take an elevator down to a bustling ground floor with a coffee shop, a grocery store, and maybe a gym or a bookstore. You've got everything you need right at your doorstep. That's the beauty of mixed-use properties!

But it's not just convenient for residents. Businesses also benefit from the built-in customer base living right above them. And from an investment perspective, these properties can be quite attractive. They offer multiple income streams and can be more resilient to market fluctuations because they're not reliant on just one type of tenant.

How to Get Started in Commercial Real Estate Investing

It's important to realize that although there are similarities between investing in commercial and residential real estate, they're not exactly the same game. Yes, the basics like doing thorough research, understanding the market, and having a solid investment strategy are crucial in both. But there are a few key differences you need to be aware of.

Now, one of the first things you might notice is that commercial properties tend to have a heftier price tag compared to residential ones. So, unless you've got a huge pile of cash lying around, you'll probably need to secure some financing. This could mean working with a bank or other lending institution or maybe even finding partners who are willing to invest with you.

Another interesting point about commercial properties is how their value is determined. Unlike residential properties, where comparable sales play a big role, the value of commercial properties is often tied directly to their income potential. In other words, how much money can this property generate? If you're looking at an office building with high occupancy rates and long-term leases, for example, that's likely to be seen as more valuable than a similar building that's half empty.

So, how do you get started? Well, a good first step is to educate yourself. Read books, attend seminars, join real estate investing groups—soak up as much knowledge as you can. Then, start looking at properties and crunching the numbers. What's the potential return on investment? What are the risks? Just like all forms of real estate investing, commercial real estate isn't a get-rich-quick scheme. It requires patience, diligence, and a keen eye for good opportunities.

Risks and Rewards of Commercial Real Estate

Let's talk about the ups and downs of commercial real estate, shall we? When it comes to rewards, commercial properties are a pretty attractive prospect. One significant point in their favor is that they can yield a higher income potential compared to residential properties. This is due to factors like larger square footage and the business nature of tenants.

You've also got the benefit of longer lease terms. When you sign a lease with a business, it's usually for a good chunk of time, which means stable, long-term income for you. Plus, dealing with businesses can sometimes be simpler than dealing with individuals. Businesses tend to be more predictable; they're less likely to abruptly break a lease, for example.

But hold up. More significant rewards can often mean more considerable risks. Commercial properties can be quite sensitive to economic conditions. For instance, a market downturn can hit commercial tenants hard, leading to higher vacancy rates and lower rents. And speaking of vacancies, when a commercial property goes vacant, filling it can take some time. It's not like renting out a house or an apartment, when you can often find a new tenant quickly. These longer vacancy periods can put a dent in your income.

And don't forget about potential maintenance nightmares. Commercial properties can host a range of activities, from the harmless to the heavy-duty industrial. This means when something goes wrong, it can go spectacularly wrong. We're talking about large-scale repairs and replacements that can seriously test your contingency funds.

Case Study: Single Tenant Struggles—A Commercial Challenge

Muhammad was the owner of a single-tenant commercial building, located in the heart of a mid-sized city. For many years, the building was home to a thriving fabric store, providing Muhammad with a steady income stream and bolstering his already impressive portfolio.

But as we all know, nothing lasts forever. The fabric store, which had been a city staple for decades, finally decided to close its doors. The once-profitable building now stood empty and silent.

Suddenly, Muhammad found himself in a predicament he had not faced before. With no tenant to pay rent, he was left footing the bill for the mortgage payments on his own. Months turned into years, and despite his best efforts, he couldn't find a new tenant to occupy the large space.

In desperation, he considered transforming the commercial property into residential units. However, after careful investigation, he realized that the cost of retrofitting the building to meet residential standards was simply too high. It just didn't make financial sense.

Muhammad then ventured into another idea. He considered dividing the vast space into a mini marketplace, allowing multiple independent vendors to sell their goods. However, even this strategy failed to turn a profit, leaving Muhammad back at square one.

(continued)

(continued)

Thankfully, Muhammad's diverse portfolio comprised several other profitable buildings. The income from these properties helped soften the blow of the loss he was facing from the vacant building. But it was a stark reminder of the risks inherent in commercial real estate investment.

Finally, after two and a half long years, a ray of hope emerged. A furniture store showed interest in the vacant space. After some negotiations and paperwork, the deal was sealed. The building once again hummed with activity and started turning a profit again.

Muhammad's experience serves as a reminder of the potential risks and rewards of commercial real estate investing. It's not always smooth sailing, and sometimes, even the best-laid plans can go awry. Many commercial investors have to be ready to weather the storms and hopefully come out stronger on the other side.

But, hey, no risk, no reward, right? Although commercial real estate can offer some pretty enticing rewards, it's also paired with its fair share of risks. It's vital to weigh these before diving headfirst into your investment journey.

Investing in Land: Unearthing Hidden Gems

Alright, let's shift gears a bit and talk about a type of real estate investing that often flies under the radar—land investing. Yes, you heard it right! Land, as in dirt, soil, terra firma. It may not sound as glamorous as flipping houses or owning big commercial buildings, but don't be fooled. Investing in land can be a lucrative venture if you play your cards right.

Land investment is exactly what it sounds like—buying a piece of land as an investment. Unlike other types of real estate, land doesn't depreciate. They're not making any more of it, after all. And although land doesn't provide rental income like buildings do, it has other ways of generating returns.

Strategies for Making Money from Land: Developing, Renting, and Selling

You can make a pretty penny from land investment in many different ways. First, there's the classic development strategy. Think of a piece of land as your canvas, and you're Picasso ready to paint a masterpiece. This could involve constructing residential homes, commercial complexes, or even getting your hands dirty with agricultural projects. The main game plan here? Boost that raw land's value by giving it a purpose, and then you can either sell it off for a tidy sum or rent out the newly developed space for a steady cash flow.

Now, if you're not ready to dive into development, there's another route you can take—renting out the land. And, no, it doesn't just mean to farmers for planting crops. You could lease it to businesses needing extra parking space or outdoor storage, or even to energy companies looking to set up wind farms or solar panels. We don't see much farmland for rent where we live in northern New Jersey, for instance, but can we pocket profits from parking lots in this bustling urban area? Absolutely!

Last, there's the method that's all about playing the long game—buying and holding. This one's pretty straightforward. You buy a chunk of land, take a deep breath, work on your patience, and wait for its value to climb. The key to success here is having a hawk-eye for areas brimming with growth potential. Once the land's value goes up, sell it off and laugh all the way to the bank. Each strategy has its own charm and challenges, so take some time to figure out which one suits your style the best.

Risks and Rewards of Land Investment

So, what are the risks and rewards of land investment? On the return side, land can offer significant profits, especially if you buy in an area before it becomes popular or if you develop the land wisely.

But, like all investments, land isn't without risks. Land doesn't always provide immediate cash flow like rental properties do, so you'll need to be prepared to cover any costs yourself, such as the mortgage, property taxes, insurance, and maintenance costs.

Plus, land can be harder to sell than buildings, especially if it's in a remote location. And if you opt for the development route, you'll have to deal with construction costs and potential regulatory hurdles.

Investing in land might not be the first thing that comes to mind when you think of real estate investing, but it can be a profitable venture if you're willing to think outside the box. As with all types of investing, the key is to do your research, understand what you're getting into, and make decisions that align with your financial goals. Happy land hunting!

The ABCs of REITs

Let's shift gears a bit and turn our attention toward a different kind of real estate investing—real estate investment trusts, or REITs. Now, I know that might sound like a mouthful, but stay with us here. By the end of this section, you'll not only understand what REITs are but also the different types available and the risks and rewards of investing in them.

What Are REITs?

Imagine being able to invest in high-value real estate properties—like shopping malls or office buildings—without having to buy the whole property yourself. Sounds pretty neat, right? Well, that's exactly what REITs allow you to do.

When you invest in a REIT, you are essentially investing in the company as a whole, not specific projects. REITs own, operate, or finance a portfolio of income-producing real estate. By purchasing shares of a REIT, you become a partial owner of all assets held by that REIT, rather than investing in individual properties or projects. The profits generated from these properties are then distributed back to shareholders in the form of dividends.

REITs are required by law to distribute at least 90% of their taxable income to shareholders as dividends, which makes them particularly attractive to investors looking for regular income.

Types of REITs: Equity, Mortgage, and Hybrid

Now, not all REITs are created equal. There are three main types of REITs: equity REITs, mortgage REITs, and hybrid REITs.

Equity REITs are the most common type of REITs and include income-generating properties such as apartments, offices, shopping centers, hotels, and warehouses. The primary source of income for these REITs is the rent collected from tenants occupying these properties. This rent is typically secured under long-term leases, providing a steady and predictable stream of income. Additionally, Equity REITs can also benefit from property value appreciation over time, which can be realized on the sale of the property. This dual-income potential makes Equity REITs an attractive investment option. However, like all investments, they carry risk, including property market fluctuations and potential vacancies.

Mortgage REITs, or mREITs, operate by lending money to real estate owners, either directly through mortgages and loans or indirectly through the acquisition of mortgage-backed securities. Their revenue is derived primarily from the net interest margin, the difference between the interest they earn on these loans and the short-term borrowing costs. In essence, mREITs act as a sort of middle broker between lenders (banks) and borrowers (property owners).

Hybrid REITs, as their name implies, incorporate elements of both equity and mortgage REITs. They own income-generating properties, much like equity REITs, and also invest in mortgages or mortgage-backed securities, paralleling the structure of mortgage REITs. This blend enables hybrid REITs to generate revenue from two streams—the rent that they collect from properties they own and the interest they earn from their mortgage investments.

Risks and Rewards of Investing in REITs

Like any investment, investing in REITs comes with its share of risks and rewards. On the plus side, REITs offer a way to invest in real estate without the need to manage properties or deal with tenants. They're also highly liquid—you can buy and sell shares in a REIT just like you would with any other stock.

REITs also offer a steady stream of income. Remember when we said that REITs are required to distribute at least 90% of their taxable income as dividends? That's a pretty attractive feature for income-focused investors.

However, the three types of REITs each come with their own unique risks.

Equity REITs

Market risk is a significant consideration for equity REITs. The value appreciation of properties can indeed enhance the returns of these REITs. However, the opposite scenario holds true as well—if property markets were to decline, the value of the properties held by the REIT could plummet, negatively affecting both its net asset value and share price.

Another risk to consider is occupancy risk. For equity REITs, rent collected from their properties serves as the primary income source. Therefore, if a considerable number of these properties were to remain unoccupied, it could significantly dent the REIT's rental income, thereby affecting its ability to distribute dividends to shareholders.

Interest rate risk, although more commonly associated with mortgage REITs, also affects equity REITs. A surge in interest rates could elevate the REIT's borrowing costs, potentially diminishing its profitability. Moreover, higher interest rates could render other less risky investments more appealing, which might provoke a sell-off of the REIT's shares, leading to a decrease in its share price.

Regulatory changes also pose a risk. Shifts in real estate laws, zoning laws, or tax regulations can have a profound impact on equity REITs. For instance, if tax laws were to change, resulting in increased taxes for REITs, it could lower their after-tax profits, thereby affecting their capacity to pay dividends.

Last, management risk is a factor that influences the performance of an equity REIT. The quality of the management team plays a crucial role. Poor managerial decisions, such as overpaying for properties or accumulating excessive debt, can have detrimental effects on the REIT's financial performance.

Investors should bear in mind these risks when considering an investment in equity REITs. However, with proper due diligence, including a thorough review of the REIT's property portfolio, its occupancy and debt levels, the quality of its management team, and the general conditions of the property markets in which it operates, investors can make an informed decision about whether or not to invest.

mREITs

Like any investment, mREITs come with their unique set of risks. First, mREITs are highly sensitive to changes in interest rates. They borrow money at short-term interest rates and lend it out at long-term rates. If short-term rates increase sharply, this can squeeze their profit margins, known as the net interest margin, and potentially cause them to cut their dividends. Conversely, a sharp decrease in long-term interest rates can result in early mortgage repayments (refinancing), forcing mREITs to reinvest at lower rates.

There's the risk of credit default. mREITs that invest in loans not backed by government agencies face the risk that borrowers may default on their loans, which could lead to significant losses.

Mortgage REITs are reliant on the broader health of the real estate market. If property values decline, this can lead to an increase in loan-to-value ratios, triggering loan defaults and leading to decreased income for mREITs.

Understanding these risks is an essential part of investing in mREITs. It's important to pay close attention to economic indicators, interest rate forecasts, and the overall health of the real estate and financial markets when considering this type of investment.

Hybrid REITs

Although the dual-income approach can potentially increase the overall returns, it comes with additional risks and complexities. On the property side, the risks are similar to those faced by equity REITs, like property market downturns or vacancies. On the mortgage side, the risks are akin to those encountered by mREITs, such as interest rate volatility and credit risk of the borrowers.

Despite these risks, hybrid REITs offer an attractive balance for investors looking to diversify within the real estate sector itself. They combine the steadiness of income from property rentals with the potential for higher but riskier returns from mortgage investments. As always, it's important for investors to thoroughly research and understand the particular hybrid REIT they are considering, including its specific mix of equity and mortgage holdings, its management team's expertise, and its track record.

And finally, overall because REITs must distribute most of their income as dividends, they often have less cash on hand to invest in growth compared to regular companies.

So, is investing in REITs right for you? Only you can answer that. But now that you understand what they are, how they work, and their potential risks and rewards, you're in a much better position to make an informed decision. And remember, diversification is key. REITs can be a valuable part of a diversified portfolio, but they shouldn't be the whole story.

Real Estate Crowdfunding: The Digital Pathway to Property Investment

Similar to REITs is real estate crowdfunding, Crowdfunding is a relatively new kid on the real estate block. If you're keen on dipping your toes into the property market but don't quite have the capital for a full-on investment, crowdfunding could be your golden ticket.

So, what is real estate crowdfunding? Imagine if you and a bunch of friends pooled your money together to buy a rental property. Now, scale that up and move it online, and voila, you've got real estate crowdfunding. It's a way for everyday people to invest in properties that would otherwise be out of reach by splitting the cost with a crowd of other investors.

How Crowdfunding Works and Its Potential Returns

Here's how crowdfunding works. Real estate crowdfunding platforms list various property projects—from residential flips to commercial developments—that are available for purchase. As an investor, you can buy a small piece of these projects, sometimes for as little as a few hundred bucks.

In terms of returns, they can come in two forms. One is regular income from rent payments if the property is leased out. The other is a share of the profits when the property is sold. The potential returns can be pretty attractive, often higher than what you'd get from traditional savings or stock market investments.

How Is Crowdfunding Different from a REIT?

The primary difference between a REIT and real estate crowdfunding lies in the level of control and liquidity. When you invest in a REIT, you're buying shares in a company that owns and manages a portfolio of properties. This provides a high level of liquidity as REIT shares can be bought and sold on major stock exchanges.

However, real estate crowdfunding enables you to invest directly into specific real estate projects. This gives you more control over your investments, as you can choose which projects to fund. However, it's typically less liquid than a REIT because your investment is tied up until the property is sold or the project is completed and profitable.

Risks and Rewards of Real Estate Crowdfunding

On the plus side, real estate crowdfunding enables you to diversify your investment portfolio without needing a ton of cash. It also gives you access to the real estate market without the headaches of being a landlord.

But, like all investments, there are risks. Real estate prices can go down as well as up, so you could lose money. And although crowdfunding platforms do their best to vet the projects they list, there's always a risk that a project could fail or underperform.

It is crucial to conduct due diligence when choosing a real estate crowdfunding platform. Some platforms might not adequately vet the projects they list, leaving investors exposed to increased risk. Shady companies might present enticing investment opportunities that seem too good to be true, often because they are. There's a very real danger of scams, mismanagement, or simply poor business practices that can result in significant financial loss. Therefore, it is paramount to research any platform thoroughly before committing your hard-earned money to an investment. Ensure that the company has a positive track record, good customer reviews, and transparent operating practices to minimize potential risk.

Real estate crowdfunding can be a great way to get into property investing. It's relatively accessible, can offer good returns, and enables you to spread your risk across multiple projects. But as with all investments, it's important to do your research and understand what you're getting into.

The Art of Wholesaling: Turning Quick Profits in Real Estate

You may have seen wholesaling all over TikTok and Instagram. It seems as if it is a new way of investing in real estate. But it's not new at all. Wholesaling is a bit different from traditional methods, but it can be a lucrative strategy if done correctly.

What Is Wholesaling?

In the realm of real estate, wholesaling is a strategy where an individual, known as a wholesaler, contracts with a seller to purchase a property and then sells the purchase contract to an end buyer. The wholesaler makes a profit from the difference between the contracted price with the seller and the amount paid by the buyer. The unique feature of wholesaling is that the wholesaler doesn't need to actually purchase the property. They simply act as the middle person between the seller and the end buyer.

To initiate a wholesale deal, the wholesaler must first locate motivated sellers. These are typically individuals who need to sell quickly due to circumstances such as financial distress, pending foreclosures, or a need to relocate. Wholesalers often find these sellers through various methods like direct mail campaigns, online advertising, or real estate investor networking events.

Once a potential property has been identified, the wholesaler negotiates a purchase price with the seller. This price needs to be low enough to allow for a profit margin when the contract is sold to the end buyer. After securing the contract at a negotiated price, the wholesaler then looks for an end buyer.

The end buyer could be a real estate investor looking for a good deal on a property to repair and resell or a homeowner looking for a house to live in. The wholesaler sells the contract to the buyer, who then completes the purchase with the original seller. The profit for the wholesaler comes from the difference between the price they contracted with the seller and the amount the end buyer pays for the contract.

Wholesaling is especially beneficial for individuals who excel at networking. This investment strategy hinges on the ability to build and maintain a wide network of contacts. On one end, wholesalers need to locate and negotiate with motivated sellers—often individuals in unique circumstances that necessitate a quick property sale. On the other end, they need to connect with potential end buyers, which can range from real estate investors seeking good deals on properties for repair and resale to homeowners in search of their next residence. Essentially, a wholesaler's success is directly tied to their networking skills, as their profit is made from the difference in price between what they negotiate with the original seller and what they secure from the end buyer. As such, those with a knack for building relationships and a wide contact base can find wholesaling a highly lucrative real estate investment strategy.

Risks and Rewards of Wholesaling

Considering the risks and rewards of wholesaling in real estate, one can identify a few key points. On the positive side, wholesaling has a relatively low barrier to entry. This is mainly due to the minimal upfront capital required compared to other real estate strategies, making it a feasible option for beginners or individuals with limited funds. Another advantage is the potential for quick returns. Unlike traditional real estate investments, which can take years to yield significant profits, wholesaling often brings profits within weeks or months. Additionally, because wholesalers don't purchase the property, they face less exposure to risks such as property damage, market downturns, or struggles in selling the property.

However, the strategy does come with drawbacks. Wholesaling is heavily dependent on finding motivated sellers and willing buyers at the same time. If a wholesaler can't secure a buyer in due time, they might need to cancel the contract or purchase the property themselves, which increases the risk. There are also legal considerations to be aware of; some states have regulations that govern wholesaling activities for consumer protection. Wholesalers need to be mindful of these laws to avoid potential legal complications. Last, because wholesalers do not retain the properties they contract, they don't accumulate assets, equity, or benefits from long-term property appreciation, which might limit their wealth accumulation in the long run.

Steps to Successful Wholesaling

Getting into wholesaling may seem appealing due to its relatively low financial barrier to entry. Many folks are eager to kickstart their real estate investing journey through wholesaling. However, it's essential to realize that it's not as straightforward as it may appear at first glance. You really need to know what you're doing. Let's take a look at the common steps for achieving success in wholesaling:

1. **Research and identify potential properties.** This is the first step in a successful wholesaling process. It involves researching and identifying potential properties that are undervalued or in distress. Tools such as Multiple Listing Service (MLS), foreclosure listings, and county records can be a good starting point.

2. **Establish contact with the property owner.** Once a potential property is identified, the wholesaler establishes contact with the owner. This can be done through direct mail, phone calls, or face-to-face meetings. The goal is to negotiate a potential deal.

3. **Secure a contract with the seller.** If the property owner is interested in selling, the wholesaler will negotiate a price and secure a purchase contract. This contract gives the wholesaler the right to buy the property at a later date, typically within a specified period.

4. **Find an end buyer.** With a contract in hand, the wholesaler then looks for an end buyer. This could be a real estate investor or a homeowner looking for a house to live in. The wholesaler can use various marketing strategies such as online listings, networking events, or direct mail to find potential buyers.

5. **Assign the contract.** Once an end buyer is found, the wholesaler assigns the contract to them for a higher price than the one agreed on with the seller. The difference in price is the wholesaler's profit.

6. **Close the deal.** The final step is to close the deal. This usually involves a closing agent who ensures that all paperwork is completed correctly, the seller gets their agreed price, and the buyer takes ownership of the property. The wholesaler gets paid their assignment fee at closing.

Mistakes to Avoid in Wholesaling

One common pitfall that rookie wholesalers often stumble on is not allocating enough time for due diligence. Some are so eager to close their first deal that they skip the crucial step of thoroughly researching the property and its potential value. This can lead to overestimating the property's worth and, consequently, agreeing to a purchase price that leaves little room for profit. To avoid this, it's crucial to invest time in comprehensive property and market analysis before signing any contract.

Another frequent misstep is underestimating the importance of networking and building relationships within the real estate community. New wholesalers may fall into the trap of thinking that finding good deals is a solo journey, when in fact, it's a highly collaborative process. Having a strong network of real estate professionals—investors, agents, contractors, and other wholesalers—can vastly improve the chances of finding profitable deals. Therefore, attending networking events, joining real estate investment clubs, and nurturing professional relationships should be high on a wholesaler's priority list.

Perhaps one of the most critical mistakes is failing to understand local real estate regulations and laws governing wholesaling. Some newbies dive into wholesaling without a grasp of the legal implications, which can lead to costly penalties and even legal action. It's essential to consult with a real estate attorney or a seasoned wholesaler to understand the legalities involved in wholesaling in your state.

New wholesalers often neglect to formulate a clear exit strategy. They might secure a contract with a seller but find themselves at a loss if they can't find an interested buyer in time. Hence, having a defined exit strategy—whether that's a list of potential buyers, the capacity to purchase the property oneself, or an agreement with a fellow wholesaler—can save a lot of stress and financial risk.

Although the world of real estate wholesaling may be painted as a quick route to wealth by many influencers on social media, we've taken the time to delve into the nitty-gritty of the strategy. We've expounded on not only the advantages but also the potential pitfalls and common errors that beginners might encounter. We did this because, all too often, those influencers tend to gloss over the potential challenges and downsides. Wholesaling, like any investment strategy, isn't a guaranteed win. It requires due diligence, networking, understanding of regulations, and a solid exit strategy.

As with any endeavor, being well informed and prepared can go a long way in minimizing risk and increasing chances of success.

■ ■ ■

We've managed to cover a vast landscape of knowledge, taking a deep dive into the multifaceted world of real estate. We unpacked the differences between residential, commercial, and land properties, each with its own unique characteristics and opportunities. And we didn't stop there; we explored the myriad ways of investing in these properties: from holding rentals, flipping houses, and commercial investing to venturing into land investments, dabbling in REITs, or joining the crowd via crowdfunding. It's been a lot to digest, but remember, as you embark on your real estate investment journey, immerse yourself in learning about the specific type of investing you choose. Knowledge is power, and in real estate, it could very well be the key to your success.

Chapter 3

Getting on the Express Bus to Your Goals

Welcome aboard! Why are we on a bus, you ask? Well, think of real estate investing as a bustling, vibrant city. There's so much to see, do, and explore. You could meander along on foot, but wouldn't it be faster to catch the express bus? That's what we're here for: to help you fast-track your understanding of real estate investing. And the best way to do that is to immerse yourself completely in real estate.

In the pages ahead, we're going to discuss the concept of immersion. Most people underestimate just how crucial immersion can be when you're venturing into something new. However, in the world of real estate, immersion serves as your training ground, helping you grasp the ins and outs of real estate investing.

Diving Head First into Real Estate

So, why is it crucial to dive headfirst into real estate investing? Well, to put it simply, immersion is the quickest and most effective way to learn. Imagine you're learning a foreign language. You could spend years studying from a book, or you could live in the country where the language is spoken. Which do you think would be more effective? Exactly. Now, apply that same logic to real estate investing. To truly understand the industry and make profitable investments, you need to immerse yourself in the market, sniff out opportunities, and learn the language of real estate.

Getting started in real estate investing can be overwhelming. You have countless paths to choose from, and it's easy to get distracted. This is where focusing your energy comes in. Just like a laser beam cuts through all the noise and concentrates its power on one point, you need to zero in on learning about real estate and become an expert in it.

An easy way to start your journey into immersion is through visualization. When you were a kid, did you ever close your eyes and imagine scoring the winning goal in a soccer match or playing the lead role in a school play? You may not have realized it then, but you were practicing visualization—a powerful tool that can help you achieve your goals. In the realm of real estate, visualization involves picturing your investment goals, imagining yourself achieving them, and keeping that image in your mind as you navigate your investing journey.

Immersing Yourself from the Start

From a young age, many of us have experienced the powerful effects of immersion. Whether it was grasping a new language faster by conversing with native speakers or mastering a musical instrument by playing in a band, these experiences attest to the fact that immersion is a potent technique that accelerates learning and comprehension. The best thing you can do is to start practicing immersive learning at a young age, but even if this is the first time you are encountering the concept, it's never too late to start.

Immersion is not merely a method, but a commitment, a profound engagement that shouldn't be underestimated. It brings a sharpened focus that enables your brainpower to be funneled into a single endeavor. When you wholly dedicate yourself to a task, you're essentially setting the stage for the magic of creation to transpire. It's akin to brewing your own potion for success. This process can be massively intensive, but the rewards are just as grand.

You might ask, why is there such an emphasis on immersion? Let's go back to our express bus analogy: immersion is the difference between hopping on a local bus versus an express bus.

Case Study: You're Never Too Young to Learn Immersion

When Noelle was just 10, all she wanted was to be a part of the children's chorus at the Metropolitan Opera House in New York City, where her mother performed as an opera singer. She was filled with dreams of joining her mom under the spotlight and sharing in the magic of the stage. Noelle auditioned, filled with hope and excitement, only to face disappointment when she did not get accepted.

She was crushed, but then, something changed. She saw an interview with a popular teen actress who had landed her dream role in a new movie. Her secret? She had fully immersed herself in the character, absorbed the storyline, and learned everything she could about the production. Inspired by the actress's approach, Noelle decided to follow suit.

Noelle threw herself into the world of opera with all her heart. She made vision boards of herself at the Met and in the performances, listened relentlessly to the music from operas featuring the children's chorus, and soaked up the history of the Met. Noelle talked about her dream with anyone who would listen. Every night, she would close her eyes and picture herself singing her heart out on that grand stage.

And then, magic happened. At Noelle's next audition, her passion and immersion shone through and she earned her place in the children's chorus. You may be wondering, "What does a child's audition have to do with real estate investing?" It's simple; they both take the same steps to success. The power of immersion helped Noelle to achieve her goals, proving that immersing oneself in a goal can be the key to unlocking it. This was Noelle's first experience with "catching the express bus." Immersion has been her North Star ever since. It may take some effort and focus, but once you're on board, nothing can stop you from reaching your destination. And just like Noelle, the earlier you learn to do this the easier achieving your goals will be.

Immersion is the express bus; it's the fast-track route to your destination. In the context of achieving your goals, it's about getting serious about your goals and bypassing the unnecessary distractions.

By immersing yourself, you foster a single-minded dedication that propels you forward, enabling you to channel all your resources and energy toward your dream. It's a demanding process, requiring both emotional and mental investment. However, the beauty lies in the fact that when you pour so much energy into something, you are bound to see results. Something has to give, and more often than not, it's the barriers that once seemed insurmountable.

So, how can you start immersing yourself in real estate? We take a look at some ways next.

How to Kickstart Your Real Estate Immersion

To start immersing yourself in real estate, the first step is to educate yourself. Read books, blogs, and research papers on real estate investment. Attend seminars, listen to podcasts, watch YouTube videos and webinars where successful investors share their experiences and insights. Don't shy away from asking questions and seeking advice.

Network

Expand your circle by networking with industry professionals. Connect with realtors, brokers, and fellow investors. Consider attending real estate investment conventions and forums, local meetups, and even virtual gatherings.

Take Classes

Consider enrolling in real estate investment courses or workshops. Many of our licensing students have no intention of becoming traditional real estate agents; they just want to learn everything they can about the real estate industry. They want to know more than all of their vendors, partners, and, of course, their competition. They take our courses on licensing, flipping and investing, building rental portfolios, construction for investors, and commercial investment. These courses provide a thorough understanding of the key concepts and techniques used in real estate investment.

Monitor the Markets

Monitor real estate market trends closely. Develop a keen understanding of market dynamics such as pricing trends, supply-demand balance, and the economic factors that affect real estate. This will be instrumental in making informed investment decisions.

Find Mentors

Identify mentors who have successful track records in real estate investing. Their advice, guidance, and feedback can prove invaluable, especially when making your first investment.

Use the Internet

Join online real estate investment forums where investors share their experiences, answer queries, and discuss investment strategies. The goal is to learn from the experiences of others.

Pour through property listings websites such as Realtor.com, Zillow, LoopNet, and Trulia. These websites provide comprehensive listings of properties, helping you understand property values, market trends, and other relevant information. Make it a habit to regularly visit the properties being rented and sold, both physically and virtually. This will give you a better understanding of what to look for in potential investment properties and help you gain practical knowledge.

Don't underestimate the value of YouTube tutorials. Many experienced real estate investors create informative video tutorials that serve as practical guides, providing step-by-step instructions and sharing valuable tips.

Listen to Podcasts

Don't overlook the value of podcasts in your immersive learning journey. Subscribing to real estate podcasts, such as Eric and Noelle's *The Real Estate Mix Video Podcast*, can be incredibly beneficial. These podcasts often feature interviews with successful investors and cover topics from property management to investment strategies. Plus, the portable nature of podcasts enables you to learn on the go. Put in your earbuds while walking the dog. Turn on your favorite show while driving to the grocery store. Podcasts are a perfect fit for busy schedules.

What Can You Do Today to Start Immersing?

By reading this book, you have already begun your journey to immersing yourself in real estate. But there are small things you can do right now, today, this week, and every day going forward to continue that journey. Start right after you put down this book.

Right now, just like 10-year-old Noelle, start visualizing! Visualization is a crucial tool on your journey. Start by visualizing your goals. What does success look like for you? Is it owning a particular property, achieving a certain return on investment, or building a rental empire, earning a specific annual income from investments? Whatever it is, keep that vision firmly planted in your mind. Visualize it regularly, and let it guide your actions.

Later today, embrace the internet rabbit hole. The internet is a wealth of information, filled with countless resources and knowledge waiting to be discovered. There's a multitude of blogs, forums, educational portals, and podcasts out there, focusing on every aspect of real estate investing. This is your playground, and you should go down this rabbit hole with an open, curious mind.

We have found immense value in online communities and forums. We actively participate in more than 100 various Facebook groups and online forums, ranging from local real estate investment communities to international property management groups. This online engagement not only supplements our ongoing learning but also enables us to form valuable connections within the industry with people we may not have met in our current circles. The internet is vast, and it can seem overwhelming, but remember, every post read, every question asked, every connection made is a step closer to your goal.

This week, find an accountability partner. This can be a mentor, a peer, or even a close friend who's also interested in real estate. Having someone to share the journey with, to discuss ideas, and to keep you accountable can make a world of difference. It adds an element of communal learning and camaraderie, making the journey less solitary and more engaging.

You can find accountability partners by joining real estate investment groups or clubs. Many local and national organizations offer memberships with access to networking events, educational seminars, and even property tours. This can be a great way to connect with like-minded individuals and learn from experienced investors in your area. Plus, the resources and events provided by such groups are often tailored specifically for real estate investors, making it an efficient use of your time and energy.

Every day, talk about real estate. In real estate, never underestimate the power of conversation. Start incorporating real estate into your everyday chatter. Whether you're at a social event, networking meeting, or even in a casual chat with friends, discuss your interests, ask questions, and share what you've learned. You'll be surprised at how much you can learn from others.

No doubt, a journey to real estate investing mastery, filled with learning, networking, and relentless market analysis, may seem daunting and exhausting. It's like standing at the foot of a mighty mountain, staring at the peak shrouded in clouds, and the path to the top feels overwhelming. However, remember that every successful journey begins with a single step. You don't have to do everything all at once. Start incorporating your learning week by week until you are up to your neck in real estate. It may require an investment of time, energy, and resources, but the rewards are truly worth the effort.

By fully committing to this process, you equip yourself with the knowledge, connections, and experience that will propel you up that mountain more swiftly than you might have thought possible.

Immersion as an Active, Dynamic Journey

Immersion in the world of real estate investing is not a passive endeavor. It requires active engagement, a curious mind, and a relentless pursuit of knowledge and opportunities. Just like Noelle's childhood dream of singing at the Metropolitan Opera House, your goals in real estate can be achieved through dedicated focus and unwavering determination.

Remember, the journey of a real estate investor is akin to catching the express bus. It's about bypassing distractions, honing your focus, and propelling yourself toward your destination. Through immersion, you tap into a wellspring of knowledge, connections, and experiences that can accelerate your growth in the industry.

So, start today. Visualize your goals, dive into the wealth of resources available, seek out like-minded individuals, and become intimately familiar with the properties and markets that interest you. Embrace every opportunity to learn, network, and explore. And above all, stay committed to your journey, for it's the dedication and persistence that ultimately lead to success.

■ ■ ■

As you embark on this immersive journey, keep in mind the words of American author Mark Twain, who once said, "Twenty years from now you will be more disappointed by the things that you didn't do than by the ones you did do. So throw off the bowlines. Sail away from the safe harbor. Catch the trade winds in your sails. Explore. Dream. Discover."

With immersion as your compass, you're not just a passenger on this bus—you're the driver of your own destiny in the world of real estate investing. So, buckle up and stay focused.

Case Study: The Real Estate Jungle—Stalking Your Prey

Eric always says, "Real estate investment is like living in the wild; you eat what you kill." So as a budding real estate investor, you must stalk your prey, metaphorically speaking. If there's a building or property you want to buy, visit it daily. Study it, get to know its strengths and weaknesses, and understand its value. This intimate knowledge will give you the upper hand when it comes time to negotiate a purchase.

Eric has an inspiring story that perfectly illustrates the power of immersion, determination, and the relentless pursuit of one's goals. This story is centered on an old, slightly run-down mixed-use property located in downtown Hackensack, New Jersey. Eric knew the moment he laid eyes on it that he was destined to own this building. There was something about it that made dollar signs appear in his eyes. Despite its evident need for restoration, he saw immense potential and knew that adding value to it would translate into a profitable investment.

Every day, he made it a point to drive past the building on his way to the office, observing it at different times and from various angles. He even assigned his team to track down the elusive property owner. They employed various methods, including scouring property tax records, using online property databases, reaching out to other local real estate agents, and even leveraging social media platforms. Despite these exhaustive efforts, they were unable to make contact.

But Eric is never one to be easily dissuaded. He held steadfast on to his vision. Knowing that buildings are his Achilles's heel, Eric was willing to go the extra mile. He began to observe the building from his parked car at different times, holding on to the belief that eventually, someone would make an appearance. His persistence paid off when one day, an older man approached the building and began to unlock the door. Seizing the moment, Eric introduced himself, alleviating the man's initial alarm and securing a meeting.

(continued)

Getting on the Express Bus to Your Goals

(continued)

Several months later, Eric's unwavering determination culminated in him becoming the proud owner of the mixed-use property. Today, it stands as one of the most profitable assets in his portfolio.

While we use the term "stalk your prey" metaphorically, of course, we in no way endorse or encourage any form of intrusive or inappropriate behavior. The essence of the phrase lies in its symbolism of relentless pursuit and unwavering focus on your goals. The story we shared of Eric encapsulates this idea perfectly. His dedication, consistency, and persistence in pursuing this property eventually led to its fruition. This narrative serves to emphasize that when you channel your energy and efforts toward a specific goal with tenacity, the universe has a way of making things fall into place. Eric's story is more than just a tale of success. It's a testament to the fruits of immersion, the power of visualization, and the relentless energy needed to manifest your goals.

Chapter 4

Recognizing Your Strengths, Weaknesses, and Ultimate Inspiration

The world of real estate investing is competitive and dynamic. Understanding one's strengths and weaknesses is not just an advantage, it's a necessity. As a real estate investor, you're not just buying properties—you're making strategic decisions, managing complex projects, and navigating a constantly changing market. Your strengths are your tools for success, enabling you to leverage your skills, knowledge, and experience to maximize returns.

However, recognizing your weaknesses provides valuable insight into areas where you can improve or seek assistance. Whether it's negotiating deals, analyzing market trends, or managing renovations, knowing where your gaps lie helps you to fill them effectively.

Beyond this, every real estate investor should understand their *ultimate inspiration*—the driving purpose behind their investment journey. This could be financial independence, providing for your family, or creating a legacy. Your ultimate inspiration acts as a compass that guides your decisions and keeps you motivated even when the market gets tough. It's the foundation on which all successful real estate investment strategies are built.

In addition to identifying your strengths, weaknesses, and your ultimate inspiration, it's equally important to assess whether you have the grit, determination, and resilience required to succeed in real estate investing. This business is not for the fainthearted. It requires a significant amount of research, financial acumen, patience, and an ability to remain calm under pressure. Market conditions can change rapidly, deals can fall through at the last minute, and unexpected costs can arise during property renovations.

By understanding your strengths and weaknesses, you can ascertain whether you possess the qualities needed to navigate these challenges. For instance, are you a problem-solver who can think on your feet? Are you patient and persistent, willing to wait for the right investment opportunity? Do you have the financial knowledge to analyze potential deals and forecast their returns? Your ultimate inspiration also plays into this. If your driving purpose is strong enough, it can provide the motivation and perseverance needed to overcome the inevitable obstacles you'll face in the real estate investment world.

Ultimately, having a clear understanding of yourself—your skills, your deficits, and your motivations—are crucial steps in determining whether you have what it takes to make it in this business. This self-awareness can help guide your investment strategy, refine your approach, and significantly increase your chances of achieving success in real estate investing. In this chapter, we walk you through the process of identifying your strengths and weaknesses. Knowing these will help you pinpoint the specific assistance you might require on your journey. We also guide you in uncovering your ultimate inspiration, the driving force behind your real estate investing dreams.

Assessing What You Have and What You Need

Picture this: you're at a huge buffet. There's everything from sushi to spaghetti, barbecue ribs to brussels sprouts. You only have one plate, and you can't possibly taste everything. You have to pick and choose. This buffet is akin to the world of real estate investing. It's vast, with an overwhelming array of options. The key to success? Knowing your palate—your strengths, weaknesses, and motivations—and choosing the dishes you're best suited for.

Why is it important to be introspective and determine what your strengths and weaknesses are? Imagine trying to eat sushi with a fork or spaghetti with chopsticks. Just as certain utensils are more suited to certain dishes, your strengths and weaknesses will naturally align you with certain areas in real estate. Your strengths will propel you forward, while recognizing your weaknesses enables you to manage them or complement them with a team that bolsters those areas.

So, how do you find out what these qualities are? Picture a real estate version of a superhero movie. In the first act, the hero discovers their superpowers. You're in that first act. Your superpowers could be anything from a knack for numbers that makes you a whiz at analyzing deals to a magnetic personality that makes networking a breeze. Unleashing your investing superpowers requires introspection, feedback from those who know you well, and a willingness to step out of your comfort zone.

Next, think about your motivation. This is your inspiration, the compass guiding your journey through the world of real estate. It could be creating a secure future for your family, achieving financial freedom, or making a difference in your community. Your inspiration is like the North Star, guiding and illuminating your path even through the darkest nights.

Last, determine your level of resilience and stick-to-itiveness. In the dynamic world of real estate investing, these are two essential qualities that can spell the difference between success and failure. This industry is riddled with challenges—fluctuating markets, financial risks, and unpredictable outcomes. It's *resilience* that enables an investor to weather these storms, to bounce back from setbacks, and to learn from mistakes. *Stick-to-itiveness,* however, fuels the determination to stay the course, even when the road gets rough. It's the quality that drives investors to keep going, to persist in their strategies, and to hold on to their investments, even when the market seems against them. Together, these traits form a formidable combination that can help any real estate investor thrive amidst adversity and, ultimately, achieve their investment goals.

Once you identify your strengths, acknowledge your weaknesses, define your motivation, and determine how resilient you are, the next step is to pull them all together. Think of these traits as the pieces of a jigsaw puzzle. All you have to do now is assemble them to form a picture that guides you into the right area of real estate investment.

Recognizing Your Strengths, Weaknesses, and Ultimate Inspiration

Case Study: Why It Is Important to Be Introspective and Determine Your Strengths and Weaknesses

Being introspective and identifying your strengths and weaknesses is akin to setting the GPS before embarking on a journey. It helps in navigating your path in real estate investment more strategically and effectively.

Consider the story of Michelle, a dynamic real estate investor who had a knack for spotting distressed properties with untapped potential. Her strength lay in her ability to visualize the transformation of these properties into profitable investments. However, she was not particularly strong in the financial analysis aspect, which often led her to underestimate renovation costs or overestimate rental income. Knowing this, she partnered with Paul, a seasoned investor with a strong financial background. Their partnership proved to be a winning combination. Michelle relied on Paul's financial acumen to ensure the numbers made sense, while Paul relied on Michelle's ability to identify properties with maximum potential. In this way, they were able to leverage their individual strengths and offset their weaknesses to make successful investments.

However, there was Juan, a highly personable investor who was excellent at building and maintaining relationships. This was particularly beneficial in his role as a landlord, as he could easily connect with and retain tenants. However, he acknowledged that he struggled with the administrative aspects of property management. Instead of letting this become a stumbling block, he outsourced these tasks to a property management company, thereby freeing up his time and energy to focus on his strength—people management.

In both these examples, the investors identified their individual strengths and weaknesses and then developed strategies to leverage their strengths and manage their weaknesses. By doing

(continued)

(continued)

so, they were able to streamline their operations, enhance their productivity, and ultimately achieve their investment goals more efficiently and effectively.

Introspection is not about dwelling on your weaknesses or simply celebrating your strengths. It's about understanding your capabilities and how to best use them. It's about acknowledging where you might need help or further learning and taking proactive measures to address these areas. Remember, in the buffet of real estate investing, the right mix of foods on your plate—your strengths, weaknesses, and motivations—can make the difference between a satisfying, nutritious meal and one that won't nourish you.

Unmasking Your Strengths and Weaknesses: An Insightful Endeavor

Unraveling your own strengths and weaknesses can often be as challenging as exploring uncharted territories. It's like attempting to read a book in which you are the main character, and you've been writing it while living it. It's so close and personal that the lines often blur, making it hard to objectively evaluate your attributes and areas of development.

So, how do you go about shining a light on these sometimes elusive traits? How do you put on the detective's hat and uncover the clues about your own strengths and weaknesses?

First, make it a point to solicit feedback from people you trust—those who know you well and will provide you with honest insights. They could be mentors, colleagues, or family members. The trick is to remember that feedback, whether positive or negative, is a gift, an opportunity for growth. It's a mirror held up for you to see your reflected self from another's perspective.

Second, step out of your comfort zone. Test your limits. This is often where you discover unknown facets of your personality and capabilities. As the saying goes, "A ship in the harbor is safe, but that's not what ships are built for." Your strengths might shine unexpectedly when you try new things, and your weaknesses may surface, giving you the chance to address them.

Last, introspect. Spend some quiet time with your thoughts. Reflect on your past experiences, victories, and failures. What were the situations where you felt most powerful and comfortable? Where did you struggle? The answers to these questions often lie in your past experiences if you take the time to dig deep and reflect.

Remember, knowing your strengths and weaknesses isn't about categorizing yourself into boxes of "good" and "bad." It's about understanding your unique attributes, your personal toolkit of skills and traits that can be honed and used in your journey of real estate investment.

Everybody discovers their strengths and weaknesses differently. Here are some ways to start the process:

- **Create two lists.** Create one for strengths and one for weaknesses. This requires a moment of truth with yourself, an exercise in honesty and objectivity. Don't shy away from the process; embrace it, for understanding your strengths and weaknesses is the first step toward optimizing your potential.

- **Talk to people you trust.** Seek the perspective of those who know you well. Their insights can reveal areas that may not be visible to you. This feedback can help you understand how others perceive your skills and where you could improve.

- **Take a personality test.** Often, these tests can unveil natural tendencies and blind spots. It's like peering into a mirror to see a reflection of your intrinsic traits. These tests often assess traits such as extroversion, introversion, openness, conscientiousness, and emotional stability. By exploring these dimensions, you can gain a deeper understanding of yourself and how you interact with others.

- **Get a coach.** A professional coach can provide objective feedback and guidance, helping you to identify and develop your strengths and navigate your weaknesses.

- **Use self-assessment tools and ask specific questions.** The digital world offers a plethora of online tools and questionnaires to evaluate your skills and areas for improvement. These can help you identify specific strengths and shortcomings that might otherwise go unnoticed. It's like using a magnifying glass to examine the intricate details of your abilities. In this chapter, we provide a short self-assessment specifically for those interested in real estate investment. It's easy and doesn't take a long time. Take the assessment to understand what areas you can improve.

This journey of self-discovery isn't about labeling yourself as "good" or "bad" in certain areas. It's about understanding and embracing your unique attributes, learning to optimize your strengths, and turning your weaknesses into opportunities for growth. The path to self-discovery is less about reaching a destination and more about enjoying the journey. As you navigate this path, remember learning about real estate is a journey, not a sprint. As you embark on this journey, embrace each step, and savor the discoveries along the way.

This activity is meant to help you figure out what you're good at and what might be a bit tricky for you. It's not a test to say whether you'll be amazing or not-so-great at real estate investing. Take us, for example: we're not math whizzes, but we've got awesome team members who are like human calculators. So, no matter what you're great at or where you might need a bit of support, there's always a way to make it work in real estate.

Real Estate Investing Self-Assessment

For each statement, answer yes or no. If you answer yes to both statements, the area might be a strength. If you answer no to one or both statements, the area might be a weakness.

Planning
- Personally and professionally, I am good at setting short-term and long-term goals.
- If given the tools, I can create a detailed business plan with actionable steps.

Organizing
- Throughout my adulthood, I have been able to manage my time effectively and prioritize tasks.
- I am able to keep track of multiple projects at once without letting pieces slip through the cracks.

Marketing
- I understand the basics of promoting a product or service.
- I have a strong understanding of social media and other platforms to attract potential clients and opportunities.

Knowledge of Neighborhoods/Regions
- I am familiar with a few different neighborhoods I would consider investing in.
- I understand the steps to research various areas to determine if they are promising for investment.

Attention to Detail
- When looking at properties, I can see past the exterior and hone in on the details of a property.
- I notice small changes in the real estate market.

(continued)

(continued)

Understanding Finances
- I have a basic understanding of how commercial and residential mortgages work.
- I am comfortable analyzing financial data and making investment decisions based on it.

People Skills
- I am comfortable talking to new people, including potential sellers and real estate agents.
- I can build strong relationships with key stakeholders.

Negotiation
- I have experience and success in putting business deals together.
- I have effectively participated in determining pricing for contracts or properties.

Construction
- I have a basic understanding of property maintenance.
- I have experience in assessing the cost and scope of potential renovations.

Creativity
- When I see a property, I can determine the potential and imagine what it can be after adding value to it.
- I am not afraid to take calculated risks in my investment strategy.

Resilience
- I can handle stress and setbacks without getting discouraged.
- I am able to bounce back quickly from failures or mistakes.

(continued)

(continued)

Research Skills

- I can effectively find properties and identify market trends and potential investment opportunities.
- I am comfortable using online resources and databases for my research.

Ethical Judgment

- I understand that there are laws regarding real estate compliance and regulations.
- I am committed to conducting business fairly, honestly, and with transparency.

Decision-Making

- I am confident in my ability to make sound decisions quickly.
- I can assess risks and rewards effectively before making an investment.

Networking

- I am comfortable building relationships within the real estate industry.
- I can leverage my network to find new investment opportunities or get advice.

Risk Management

- I understand the potential pitfalls involved in real estate investment.
- I can develop strategies to mitigate these risks.

Patience

- I understand that real estate investment can be a slow process and I'm prepared for that.
- I can wait for the right opportunity rather than rushing into poor investments.

(continued)

(continued)

Understanding of Laws and Regulations

- I'm familiar with laws and regulations related to real estate in my area.

- I'm willing to learn and stay updated on changes to these laws and regulations.

Customer Service

- I can handle inquiries and complaints from tenants professionally.

- I'm committed to providing a good living experience for my tenants.

Adaptability

- I can adapt my strategies based on changes in the market.

- I'm open-minded and ready to explore new trends in real estate investment.

Understanding Your Ultimate Inspiration

Understanding your ultimate inspiration behind venturing into real estate investing is as important as identifying your strengths and weaknesses. It's the fuel that keeps you moving forward, the beacon that guides your decisions, and the framework that shapes your strategies.

Is it financial freedom that you seek? You may be looking for a way to earn income while also having the freedom and flexibility to set your own schedule. Some individuals thrive in high-pressure situations and enjoy the challenges that come with real estate investing. It requires quick thinking, problem-solving skills, and adaptability, which can be exciting and fulfilling for those who are up for the challenge.

Regardless of your specific motivations, real estate investment offers countless opportunities for growth, learning, and success. With the right mindset and determination, you can turn your weaknesses into strengths and achieve your goals. Always keep an open mind.

Real Estate Investing Ultimate Inspiration Self-Assessment

For each statement, answer yes or no. Be honest with yourself. Your answers can help you to figure out your ultimate inspiration. You can have more than one inspiration, but eventually, one or two will ring more true with you than the others.

Financial Freedom
- I want to make enough money through real estate investing to cover all my bills.
- I am interested in building wealth through real estate investing.

Time Freedom
- I want to have the freedom to control my own schedule.
- I hope that real estate investing will allow me more time for personal interests or hobbies.

Work-Life Balance
- I am looking for a better work-life balance than my current job provides.
- I believe real estate investing can provide me with the flexibility to spend more time with family and friends.

Escape the Nine-to-Five
- I do not want to be tied to a traditional nine-to-five job.
- I am motivated by the idea of earning income without being tied to a desk or specific working hours.

Be Your Own Boss
- I want to be my own boss and make my own decisions.
- I am attracted to the autonomy and control that come with running my own real estate business.

(continued)

(continued)

Wealth Accumulation

- I want to accumulate wealth to provide a comfortable lifestyle for myself and my family.

- I see real estate as a key part of my strategy for long-term wealth creation.

Retirement Planning

- I am looking at real estate investing as a way to secure a comfortable retirement.

- I want to build a portfolio of properties that will provide income during my retirement years.

Legacy Building

- I want to create a legacy that I can pass down to future generations.

- I view real estate investing as a way to make a lasting impact on my family's future.

Do You Have What It Takes to Be a Real Estate Investor?

Remember Eric's determination story in Chapter 3? When he practically turned into a private investigator to get a hold of that downtown Hackensack, New Jersey, building owner. His story is a classic example of what we like to call *stick-to-itiveness*: having the grit and gumption to hang on to your dreams like a dog with a bone. It's about refusing to take no for an answer, always keeping your eye on the prize, and staying committed to your vision come hell or high water. It's about rolling up your sleeves, being ready to put in the elbow grease every single day, and sticking it out, even when things seem impossibly tough.

Now, we're not going to sugarcoat it—real estate investment isn't a walk in the park. The path to success is often littered with obstacles, disappointments, and downright failures. Deals can evaporate into thin air, markets can nosedive, and renovation costs can skyrocket out of nowhere. It's all too easy to feel disheartened and want to throw in the towel.

But here's the thing—if you've got stick-to-itiveness, you'll see these challenges differently. Instead of stumbling blocks, they become stepping-stones on your journey to success. Each no you hear? That's just getting you one step closer to a yes. Every failure? Just another lesson that brings you closer to success.

So, how do you develop this superpower, you ask? Well, that's the million-dollar question, isn't it?

Developing Stick-to-Itiveness

Developing that tenacious quality of stick-to-itiveness takes deliberate practice. It requires time, patience, and a whole lot of practice. Let's dive deeper into how someone could go about building this invaluable trait.

First, it all begins with setting clear, well-defined goals. Imagine a person named Alex, who has decided to venture into real estate investment. Alex doesn't just say, "I want to invest in real estate." Instead, he outlines SMART (specific, measurable, achievable, relevant, time-bound) goals. This might look something like, "I want to purchase my first rental property within the next six months." By doing so, Alex gives himself a clear target to aim for and a way to measure his progress.

Now, as Alex embarks on this journey, he's bound to encounter obstacles. But here's where stick-to-itiveness comes into play. Instead of viewing these challenges as setbacks, Alex sees them as stepping stones toward his goal. Every hurdle he overcomes is another lesson learned, another step closer to success.

Persistence is the fuel that keeps Alex moving forward. Even on days when everything seems to be going wrong, Alex stays the course. He continues to do the work, day in and day out, even when he'd rather do anything else. That's the essence of stick-to-itiveness—pushing through, even when the going gets tough.

But let's not forget the power of a positive attitude. Despite the challenges, Alex remains optimistic. He keeps his eyes on the prize, maintaining a positive outlook that helps him navigate through the rough patches. This unwavering belief in his vision is a crucial part of cultivating stick-to-itiveness.

And then there's commitment. Alex doesn't just dip his toes in the water; he dives in headfirst. He's committed to his goal and willing to do whatever it takes to get there. His commitment is what keeps him going, even when the journey gets tough.

Of course, nobody achieves their goals in isolation. Alex surrounds himself with a supportive network—people who understand his vision, cheer him on, and offer advice when he needs it. This support system is invaluable in keeping Alex motivated and focused on his goal.

Finally, Alex understands the importance of celebrating small victories. Every step forward, no matter how small, is progress. So, he takes the time to acknowledge these small wins. They serve as a reminder of how far he's come and motivate him to keep going.

There you have it. The journey to developing stick-to-itiveness isn't always easy, but with patience, persistence, and a dash of positivity, it's definitely achievable.

Making It a Family Affair

Eric and Noelle have made family involvement a cornerstone of their business ventures. Both understand the importance of teamwork and the value of diverse perspectives. They routinely seek advice from their spouses, Lina and David, respectively, on key business decisions, fostering an environment of collaboration and mutual respect.

Moreover, they extend this inclusive approach to their children as well. Noelle's son and stepson, Brendan and Harold, often accompany her to the office. Despite being tweens, the boys are an integral part of the business, taking on responsibilities such as filing, shredding papers, setting up for events, and conducting internet research. Not only does this involvement teach them important skills but also it instills in them a sense of responsibility and pride in contributing to the family business.

Similarly, Eric brings his 10-year-old daughter, Emma, to the office to help out and even brought his teenage son, Ethan, into the fold, having him work with their real estate brokerage for an entire summer. This hands-on experience provided both Emma and Ethan with invaluable insights into the world of real estate investing and enabled them to contribute meaningfully to the family business.

For Eric and Noelle and their families, business isn't just about profits and growth; it's about working together as a family unit, learning from each other, and building something meaningful together. Now, let's look at how you can get your family involved and on board with your journey into real estate investing, just like Noelle and Eric did. The following sections outline steps you can take to involve your family in the process and making them feel like part of the team.

Practice Open Communication

Initiate an open conversation with your family about your plans. Explain why you're interested in real estate investing—whether it's for financial growth, building a legacy, or simply pursuing a new challenge. Let your family in on your ultimate inspiration and talk about how it affects them. Be transparent about the benefits as well as the risks involved. Real estate investing can be time-consuming and may have financial implications that could affect the whole family. By being open and honest, you set realistic expectations and help your family understand what they're signing up for.

Teach the Basics

The world of real estate investing can be complex. It's important to educate your family about the basics so they can understand what you're getting into. Share resources like books, podcasts, and articles. Consider setting up weekly or biweekly family learning sessions where you can discuss these resources and how they apply to your situation. Noelle's son frequently listens to their podcast and can explain basic investing concepts to his tween friends. This will not only increase their knowledge but also foster a sense of teamwork.

Include Your Family in Decision-Making

Involve your family in the decision-making process. When considering a potential property, ask for their input. Encourage your children to research the neighborhood or nearby schools and amenities, and involve your spouse in budgeting and financial planning. This inclusion shows them that their opinions are valued and that they're an integral part of the venture.

Maintain Balance

Although your new venture is exciting, it's essential to maintain balance. Make sure that your real estate investment activities don't consume all your family's time and energy. Allocate time for family activities and relaxation, showing them that while the investment is important, it's not going to overshadow family life.

Celebrate Every Win

When the Center for Real Estate Education has a big win, Noelle brings home a special cake or pie to celebrate with the whole family and let them in on the success. Celebrate every win with your family, no matter how small. Whether it's finalizing the purchase of a new property, securing a great tenant, or making a profit for the first time, make sure everyone feels part of these successes. This not only reinforces the positive aspects of real estate investing but also helps to keep the family motivated and involved in the process.

Assign Roles

If appropriate, consider assigning roles to each family member based on their ages, skills, and interests. One family member could be responsible for researching potential properties, another could take charge of financial planning, and another could manage interactions with tenants. This can give everyone a sense of ownership and responsibility in the project.

Conduct Regular Check-Ins

Keep the lines of communication open throughout the process, especially with your spouse or significant other. Regularly check in with your family to discuss how things are going, address any concerns, and celebrate progress. This can help to keep everyone engaged and invested in the process.

Lead by Example

Show your family what stick-to-itiveness looks like. Show up every day, do the work, stay positive, and never give up. Your actions will speak louder than your words.

When you include your family in your real estate investing journey, it's like giving them a backstage pass to the show. They get to see firsthand the long hours, the attention to detail, and the dedication that goes into making investment decisions. It's no longer just "Mom or Dad is working late again." Instead, they understand why you're burning the midnight oil, why you're so focused, and why this venture matters so much to you. It's a shared journey, a collective effort, and this understanding can bring you closer as a family.

The Makings of Amazing Investors

As you reflect on the insights gained from this chapter, remember that you're embarking on a transformative journey. Just as a skilled chef selects ingredients to create a masterpiece, you're assembling your unique combination of strengths, motivations, purposes, and resilience to craft your success in real estate investing.

The stories of Michelle and Juan serve as powerful reminders that recognizing and embracing your strengths and weaknesses is a strategic move, not a sign of weakness. It's a conscious choice to maximize your potential and achieve remarkable results.

Unmasking your strengths and weaknesses might feel like navigating uncharted territory, but it's a crucial step toward becoming a proficient real estate investor. Remember, feedback is a gift, and stepping out of your comfort zone is where growth happens. Your past experiences hold valuable clues to your capabilities.

Whether you prefer creating lists, seeking feedback, taking personality tests, or using self-assessment tools, the goal remains the same: to uncover the unique attributes that will guide your journey. Embrace this process, for it's the cornerstone of realizing your full potential.

■ ■ ■

Real estate investment isn't for the faint of heart. It requires research, financial acumen, patience, and an ability to stay calm under pressure. Deals can change in a heartbeat, and unexpected costs can arise during renovations. That's why it's crucial to understand if you have what it takes.

Remember, stick-to-itiveness is a superpower in this field. It's about refusing to take no for an answer, always keeping your eye on the prize, and staying committed to your vision come hell or high water. With persistence, a positive attitude, and a strong support system, you can overcome any obstacle.

And if you're bringing your family along for the ride, make sure to communicate, educate, and involve them in the process. Celebrate wins together and maintain balance between your investment endeavors and family life.

As you explore real estate investment, let your ultimate inspiration be your compass. Whether it's financial freedom, time freedom, work-life balance, or any other driving force, keep it at the forefront of your decisions. Your ultimate inspiration will be the steadfast foundation on which you build your success.

Chapter 5

Before You Buy, Know the Why

The world of real estate investing is as vast as it is complex, offering myriad opportunities for wealth creation and financial freedom. However, the path to success in this field is not always straightforward. The journey can be fraught with challenges, risks, and uncertainties that could potentially derail even the most ambitious investment plans. This is why it's so important to fully understand what you're getting into before you take the plunge.

This chapter encapsulates a fundamental principle of successful real estate investing. It emphasizes the importance of having a clear understanding of your investment goals and the specific reasons why a certain property might help you achieve those goals. This principle serves as a compass to guide you through the sometimes muddy waters of real estate investing, ensuring that every decision you make is purposeful, strategic, and aligned with your overall objectives.

So far, we've helped you uncover your ultimate inspiration—the driving force behind your desire to venture into the world of real estate. Be it the desire for wealth creation, the longing for more quality time with your family, or the burning desire to be your own boss, we helped you uncover your motivations. However, the why we're about to explore in this chapter is a different beast altogether. This why isn't about your overarching life goals. Instead, it's about the tactical, strategic reasons that dictate why a specific property, in a specific location, at a specific price fits into your investment strategy. It explores the logistical and the practical considerations that guide the choices you make as a successful real estate investor. This why is what navigates you through the specifics of each investment decision, ensuring every step is toward profitability. This why is equivalent to your *professional goal*.

Knowing your why is just the beginning. To make informed investment decisions, you need to investigate several key aspects of real estate investing, from understanding your investment goals to researching the real estate market, evaluating specific properties, conducting a thorough financial analysis, and considering legal and regulatory implications.

In real estate investing, as in life, knowledge is power and your why is your knowledge. The more you know about a potential investment, the better equipped you'll be to navigate the challenges and capitalize on the opportunities that come your way.

Understanding Your Investment Goals

Before you even think about investing your hard-earned money or other people's money (OPM) in a potential property, you must get clarity on your investment goals. Your goals will guide you through the choppy waters of real estate. Each investor's goals are unique, as diverse as the individuals themselves. Some investors may be drawn to the steady stream of passive income that rental properties can provide, relishing the prospect of building a reliable revenue stream that beats traditional retirement plans. Others may seek the thrill and potential high returns of flipping properties, buying low, renovating, and selling high. Still others may have their sights set on the long-term value appreciation, playing the patience game and waiting for the market to work its magic, turning their investment into a golden nest egg.

The beauty of real estate investing lies in its versatility. It can cater to different goals, and there is a strategy out there that aligns with each one. The key is to identify what you hope to achieve through your investments and then align your strategy accordingly.

Assessing the Type of Investor You Are

Many of our students are amazed to realize how much of becoming a real estate investor is self-reflection. Your why is basically another way to say your professional investment goals. To establish your professional real estate investment goals, you first need to undertake some serious introspection, followed by a healthy dose of industry research. You've already started embarking on the enlightening journey of self-exploration by assessing your strengths and weaknesses in the previous chapters. It's time now to channel that newfound understanding of yourself toward shaping your professional goals in real estate investment. You must be wondering what type of investor you are destined to be. The answer largely depends on your self-knowledge, time commitment, and risk tolerance.

Successful real estate investing begins with introspection. Think about the strengths that you identified in Chapter 4. Consider the skills and knowledge you recognized and how they align with the demands of real estate investing. What did you discover as your core competencies? Perhaps you have a knack for deciphering volatile market trends or a deep understanding of the legal and financial nuances in property transactions. Maybe your expertise lies in identifying properties with untapped potential and envisioning their transformation. Each of these skills plays a critical role in real estate investing, and matching your identified strengths to your skills is the first step toward leveraging them effectively.

Consider your time commitment. Real estate investing is not a passive endeavor; it requires active involvement. Are you prepared to dedicate time to managing properties, dealing with tenants, and maintaining buildings? If you don't have the time or inclination for these tasks, you might want to opt for less demanding investment strategies or consider hiring a property manager.

Last, assess your risk tolerance. Every investment comes with a degree of risk, and real estate is no exception. Are you comfortable taking on debt to finance purchases? Are you prepared to weather market fluctuations? Understanding your own comfort level with risk will help inform which strategies you choose to pursue.

Once you've done this self-evaluation, the next step is to understand the real estate investment strategy that fits your investment goals best. Research different real estate markets, types of properties, and investment strategies. Arm yourself with information and use it to identify your professional goals.

Choosing Your Real Estate Investment Strategy

Embarking on the self-reflective journey detailed in the previous section equips you with the insights needed to choose your investment strategy wisely. Whether it's flipping houses, buying and holding, investing in commercial or residential properties, venturing into REITs, or even buying land, your decision depends heavily on your individual goals, time commitment, and risk tolerance.

Flipping properties, for instance, might appeal to those seeking an active role, ready to roll up their sleeves and get involved in property renovation. It's a strategy that demands time, energy, and a keen eye for potential—but the rewards can be considerable when executed well.

However, buying and holding properties might be the perfect fit for those who value steady, long-term returns. This approach enables you to reap the benefits of consistent rental income and potential property appreciation over time, especially for those with a lower risk appetite.

When it comes to choosing between residential or commercial properties, consider your market knowledge and comfort zone. Residential properties often require less initial capital and can be easier to understand for first-time investors. However, commercial properties often offer higher yield and longer lease agreements, making them an attractive option if you're willing to navigate a more complex market.

Considering REITs? This could be an excellent choice if you're interested in real estate but prefer a more hands-off approach. REITs offer the opportunity to invest in a diverse range of properties without the need for direct management, ideal for those with limited time.

Finally, land investments can offer significant potential returns, particularly in areas of high development. However, they may also require a higher risk tolerance and a keen understanding of zoning laws and future development plans.

This introspective process and understanding of market dynamics guide your decision-making process. It empowers you to choose the strategy that not only aligns with your professional goals but also resonates with your strengths, commitment level, and risk tolerance.

Case Study: From Commercial Dreams to Residential Success

A great example of merging your ultimate inspiration, your strengths and weaknesses, and your professional why is the story of Max and Edward, a married couple from Pennsylvania who shared a passion for real estate investing. At first, they were really excited about the idea of making big profits by investing in commercial properties. They imagined a future filled with large lucrative deals. But then they took a step back and thought about things more carefully.

You see, Max and Edward had saved up $250,000 together. It was a decent amount of money, but they realized it wasn't nearly enough to buy the expensive commercial properties they were interested in without taking out a large, complicated mortgage. After doing some research, they found out that the properties they wanted in their city cost millions of dollars. Plus, they realized that they were really good at connecting with people and fixing up houses, skills that are more valuable in the residential real estate market.

But the most important thing they realized was that they didn't just want to make quick money. They had a bigger dream in mind. They wanted to build a portfolio of properties that would bring in a steady income. That way, they could spend more time with their kids and their aging parents. So, they did the math and figured out that they could afford to buy a small multifamily fixer-upper home for about $200,000, which fit their budget and long-term goals much better.

This new insight made them change their strategy. Instead of stretching their money thin trying to buy commercial properties, they decided to buy a small multifamily home outright. They used their savings to do that and had $50,000 left over for repairs and improvements to make the property more valuable and generate more rental income.

(continued)

(continued)

As time went on, they were able to refinance the property and take out some of the equity to invest in more properties. It might have seemed like they were taking a step back, but, in reality, they were making a big leap toward their ultimate vision.

Max and Edward's journey in real estate took an exciting turn when they started getting to know their tenants. They found a lot of satisfaction in providing comfortable and well-maintained homes for their tenants, which created a sense of community. Their natural ability to connect with people was not only helpful in negotiations but also in building strong relationships with their tenants.

Because they were good at fixing things around the house, they were able to take care of minor repairs themselves, which saved them money and made their tenants happy. For bigger repairs, they hired reliable professionals to keep their properties in great shape.

Over time, their smart investments paid off, and the steady income from their properties became their financial foundation. This enables them to achieve their dream of spending more quality time with their family. Their story shows us that in real estate investing, it's not just about chasing the biggest profits. It's about finding a path that matches your skills and goals. Max and Edward's journey started with some self-reflection and careful planning, proving that a well-defined goal can guide investors to success.

Choosing the right property type and location is a crucial part of this alignment. For instance, if your goal is rental income, you'd want a property in an area with high rental demand, like near a university or a thriving business district. But, if you're into flipping, a developing neighborhood or a distressed property in an otherwise attractive area could be the perfect canvas for your project. If long-term value appreciation is what you're after, you might want to consider locations with promising future growth.

Your real estate investment strategy is not just about the what, but more importantly, the why. Once you're clear about your why, the what, where, and how become much easier to figure out. So, take a moment to reflect on your goals. They will guide you to your treasure.

It's easy to get swept up in the excitement of buying a big, fancy commercial building. But remember, investing in real estate is not a love affair—it's a business decision. Resist the temptation to make an impulse purchase driven by emotion. Instead, base your investment choices on thorough research, careful analysis, and concrete data, like Max and Edward did. Understand the market dynamics, study the property's financials, and evaluate the potential returns. A successful investor doesn't fall in love with a property; they fall in love with the numbers.

Researching the Real Estate Market

The thrill of discovering a new property can be exhilarating. The allure of its charm, the promise of its potential, the vision of what it could become—it's enough to make anyone's heart race. But here's the catch: real estate investing isn't about collecting beautiful properties; it's about making strategic business decisions. It's not a romantic pursuit, but a calculated endeavor. Think of it as a chess game, where every move counts and strategy is key.

It's easy to let your emotions take the wheel when you're faced with a beautifully staged home or a property that checks all your personal preferences. The hardwood floors, the view from the balcony, the cozy fireplace—these features might tug at your heartstrings, but they shouldn't dictate your investment decisions. Impulse purchases driven by emotion, much like impulse buys at the supermarket, often lead to regret. That candy bar might look tempting, but it doesn't align with your health goals. Similarly, an attractive house might seem appealing, but if the numbers don't add up, it won't align with your investment goals. To help you to determine the why, evaluate the reasons why a specific property, in a specific location, at a specific price, fits into your investment strategy. Base your choices on hard facts and thorough research:

- **Understand the market dynamics.** Is it a buyer's market or a seller's market?
- **Study the property's financials.** Does the rental income cover the mortgage payments and maintenance costs?
- **Evaluate the potential returns.** What is the projected appreciation rate?

Although it's natural to feel a certain emotional pull toward a property, always let the facts lead the way. Let your head guide your heart, not the other way around. Remember, in the world of real estate investing, it's not about finding a property you can live in; it's about finding a property that will grow your investment portfolio.

Picture this: you've just discovered a property that seems perfect. It's got everything you want, and it's right in the area you've been eyeing. But wait, don't sign on the dotted line yet. It's important to ask some key questions before you make your move. For instance, why this property? Have you compared it to others in the neighborhood? Maybe there's another property just around the corner that's even better suited to your investment goals.

But what if you've been handed an exclusive off-market opportunity? Those situations are very tempting. You know there are 50 other investors chomping at the bit for this chance. But hold on! Don't get swept up in the exclusivity. Make sure it aligns with your strategy first.

And then there's the property with untapped potential. Yes, it's just a small house now but imagine a five-story apartment building in its place. The zoning laws already allow it. But are you ready for that kind of project? Do you have the resources to take it on?

Or maybe you've heard some juicy news at a town council meeting. A big company is moving in, bringing a wave of workers who'll need somewhere to live. That's great news for rental demand, but have you considered the competition? Will you be able to offer something that they can't?

Writing Your Own Story of Success

When you're on the hunt for your next investment, think of each property as a book in a library. Although every book has its own story, not all are going to be bestsellers. The art lies in discovering the plot that resonates with your investment narrative.

The cover of your book, the location, is often the first thing that catches your eye. Is it an urban epic, set in a bustling city center? Or perhaps nestled in a peaceful suburb? What future plots are being developed in the area? The setting of your story can significantly influence its climax and ending.

As you look into the chapters, the rental yield and potential for value appreciation tell the kind of tale you're reading. A high rental yield might suggest a fast-paced thriller, filled with immediate action, while a property with a strong potential for value appreciation could be like a gripping suspense novel, keeping you on the edge of your seat as its true worth gradually unfolds.

But don't overlook the importance of the supporting characters—local amenities, crime rate, school district, public transport access, and job market. These elements add depth to your story, enhancing or detracting from the appeal of your book.

Now, consider the condition of the book. Is it a well-worn paperback, a fixer-upper in a sought-after neighborhood? This could be an undervalued classic. But remember, this journey of transformation requires time, skills, and a budget for renovations.

However, a glossy hardcover with a high rental yield but located in a crime-ridden area might seem like an great mystery novel at first glance. But beware, it could turn out to be a horror story, with unknown challenges lurking around every corner.

As you navigate the library of real estate, take the time to read each book carefully. Analyze its plot, assess its characters, and align its narrative with your own investment goals. Only then will you be able to identify the true bestsellers among the shelves of ordinary tales.

We can't stress enough that real estate investing is every bit like a chess game. Every move should be strategic, calculated, and emotion-free. Many investors fall in love with properties, but the successful ones fall in love with the numbers and the potential for a solid return on their investment!

Understanding Market Trends

Market trends in real estate refer to the patterns, shifts, and changes that occur in the real estate market over time. These trends can encompass various aspects, including property prices, supply and demand, interest rates, economic conditions, and consumer preferences. By analyzing market trends, real estate professionals and investors gain insights into where the market is headed, helping them make informed decisions about buying, selling, or investing in properties. It's like reading the market's pulse to understand its current and future health, enabling you to make decisions based on what's likely to happen next.

To understand the market trends, you need to keep tabs on demographic shifts, economic indicators, and real estate market cycles. Imagine you're thinking about making a real estate investment in a neighborhood. Now, picture this: a trendy tech startup chooses to call that very neighborhood home. What does this mean for your investment strategy?

- **Demographic shift.** You can anticipate a change in the types of people flocking to the area. With a tech startup moving in, you're likely to see a surge in young professionals. These folks are usually on the lookout for convenient and stylish living spaces. Mixed use, multifamily apartment properties may do well in this environment.

- **Economic indicator.** The arrival of the tech startup is a strong indicator signaling economic growth. It often comes with job opportunities and higher incomes for the residents. This is a positive economic indicator for the neighborhood.

More jobs and better wages mean increased demand for housing. Economic indicators such as unemployment rates and income levels play a crucial role. If the economy is doing well and people have disposable income, they're more likely to invest in buying houses, so flips may be best. But when the economy is in a downturn, many people wait to buy and decide to save money by renting. This could drive up rental rates, making a buy and hold investment even more valuable.

- **Real estate market cycle.** You're entering the real estate market, and it's important to know if you're catching a wave or if you're already riding it. In this case, the tech startup's arrival could signify the start of an upswing in the neighborhood's real estate market cycle. Prices might not have peaked yet, and there's potential for growth. So, it's a good time to consider your investment. There are periods of growth when the market is hot and periods of slowdown when it cools off. Knowing which phase you're in can help you decide if it's the right time to buy, sell, or hold.

By keeping an eye on these factors—demographic shifts, economic indicators, and market cycles—you can make more informed decisions in real estate investing. In this scenario, it's about recognizing the opportunity that comes with the tech startup's presence and aligning your investment strategy with the changing dynamics of the neighborhood.

You should also consider supply and demand dynamics. Are new businesses popping up in your chosen area? What about property prices—are they steadily climbing or have they hit a standstill? These factors can offer valuable insights into potential opportunities or risks.

To track property prices and rental rates, you need to become a detective of the real estate market! Public records reveal previous sale prices, tax histories, and even the owner's identity. Real estate websites, like Zillow and Trulia, offer a wealth of data right at your fingertips, including current asking prices and rent estimates.

To get hyperlocal, you can engage a real estate agent who knows the area like the back of their hand. They can provide valuable insights into realistic pricing and rental trends based on firsthand experience. Don't forget to also check classified ads in local newspapers and online platforms. The key to success lies in regularly monitoring the market. This will ensure you stay ahead of the curve and seize the most exciting opportunities before they even hit the mainstream radar.

We talk a lot about looking local—the micro market. But you must also keep an eye on the bigger picture: national trends. Even though they might seem far removed from your local market, they often have a trickle-down effect. So, whether interest rates are skyrocketing, or the overall economy is in a slump, these factors can impact your local market.

One of the most effective ways to stay informed is through trusted financial news sources like CNBC, Bloomberg, or *The Wall Street Journal*. They serve up daily doses of market trends, economic forecasts, and real estate news. Subscribing to their newsletters or alerts gives you a front-row seat to the latest happenings.

Equally valuable are real estate–specific publications like Realtor.com, Zillow's research page, GlobeSt.com, or Inman.com. They also give a macro-focused picture while offering a deep dive into the nuances of the property market, arming you with the insights you need to make informed investment decisions.

Don't overlook economic reports, either. Resources like the US Bureau of Labor Statistics, the Federal Reserve's Beige Book, and the US Census Bureau's housing data provide a wealth of information on employment trends, regional economic conditions, and housing statistics. You may not look at these macroeconomic indicators every day or even every month, but keeping an eye on them can lead you through the landscape of the national economy.

Remember, staying informed isn't a one-off task—it's a continuous endeavor. Set aside time each day to catch up on the latest news and review market trends. This consistent effort ensures that you're always equipped with up-to-date knowledge, ready to seize golden opportunities as they arise.

Evaluating a Potential Property

You found your ultimate inspiration, you know all of your strengths and weaknesses, and you know your why; now a residential property has caught your eye, and you want to move on it. But wait! Before you run to the bank, you must do an in-depth property evaluation.

Location, Location, Location!

Location is the heart and soul of real estate investing. Just like gold prospectors in the old west, you're on a quest to strike gold—not in the form of nuggets, but in prime real estate locations. Your mission is to find that one spot that aligns perfectly with your investment strategy and goals.

If you're aiming for a younger, more dynamic demographic like millennials or Gen Z, your search should be in vibrant neighborhoods. These areas are usually characterized by their lively atmosphere, unique and quirky local businesses, and a strong sense of community. Think of places that blend cultural richness and modern living. They often offer a mix of trendy eateries, bustling farmers markets, a thriving arts scene with edgy art galleries, stylish music venues, and craft cocktail bars.

However, if your target market is families seeking tranquility and a strong sense of community, serene suburban areas might be your sweet spot. Research places that offer the peaceful environment families often look for. Areas with lush parks, family-friendly amenities, and quality schools and that are away from the hustle and bustle of city life would be the best for your investment.

Location is probably one of the most important factors to consider when evaluating a potential property. For example, take Richard, an investor from the West Coast who purchased a low-priced Victorian house. He invested heavily in renovations, transforming it into a truly stunning property. However, he was so excited about the deal he got on the house, he overlooked the house's location in a high-crime neighborhood. Despite its beauty and amenities, potential buyers were wary to spend so much money in an area with safety concerns. Richard learned the hard way that the best property in a bad location is always a bad investment. This experience made him prioritize location in all his future investments.

The best property in a less-than-ideal location is always a questionable investment. Eric always says, "You can renovate a house, but you can't change its location." So, whether you're looking for the hippest spot in town or a tranquil suburban retreat, always let the location lead the way.

Structural Soundness

The next step in your property evaluation is to give your potential investment a thorough checkup. You need to examine the bones of the building—because in the case of successful real estate investing, it's what's on the inside that counts.

The foundation is the backbone of your property; it's what keeps the whole structure upright. You want to make sure that it's solid. Look for any signs of cracking or sinking. If the doors and windows are sticking or there are visible cracks in the walls or floors, it might be a sign of foundation issues. A house with a shaky foundation won't stand the test of time.

Are the walls sturdy? Are they standing strong and proud, or do they wobble like jelly? Tap them, push them, knock on them, listen to them. If they sound hollow or feel unstable, they might need some serious attention.

Now, while you're at it, keep an eye out for signs of dampness or cracks. Dampness can be a silent killer in homes. It's like the flu for buildings—it starts small, but if left untreated, it can cause major structural damage. Look for dark water spots, peeling paint, or a musty smell. And cracks? They are like the wrinkles of a building, except they aren't a sign of wise aging but of potential structural issues.

A property with good bones can save you a ton of money and headaches down the line. So, grab your magnifying glass and start investigating!

Essential Amenities

Let's take a casual walk through our potential property. What are we looking for? It's important to inspect all the rooms—bedrooms, bathrooms, kitchens, and living areas.

First, consider the bedrooms and bathrooms. You don't want too many or too few. Ask yourself, is there enough space for a family to live comfortably? If you're targeting young professionals, are there enough rooms for roommates? Bedrooms increase property value, and bathrooms are a necessity. For example, Margaret owned a three-bedroom house that wouldn't sell due to its single bathroom. After months of no success, she decided to invest in adding a half bath. Converting an underused closet into a compact bathroom, the house quickly caught buyers' attention. Margaret's decision to add the half bath not only sold the house but also reinforced the importance of understanding buyers' needs. A family that needs three bedrooms definitely needs more than one bathroom.

Next, evaluate the kitchen. The kitchen is the heart of the home for most families. Think of the time you have spent sitting around your kitchen, having great conversation while either watching someone cook or cooking by yourself. To many people the kitchen is a deal breaker. Does it have modern appliances, plenty of counter space, and storage? Or does it appear outdated? If it doesn't meet your standards the kitchen may be where you focus a significant amount of your rehabilitation money. A well-equipped kitchen often sways buyers and renters in favor of a property.

While examining the living area, pose a few critical questions to yourself: Does its size correspond with the capacity of the bedrooms? Can it comfortably host a family movie night or a social gathering? A living area that's too small can lead to discomfort. It's crucial to have a space where individuals can unwind and feel a sense of belonging.

Also, look out for additional features that could increase value. For example, a fireplace isn't a necessity, but it can make a property feel homey during cold winter nights. Similarly, a patio or backyard, although not essential, can enhance the appeal of a property.

It provides an outdoor space for activities like summer barbecues, sunbathing, or enjoying a cup of coffee in the morning.

As you peruse the property, remember to look beyond the surface. Uncover the potential, spot the opportunities, and envision what could be. After all, a house isn't just a building; it's a home waiting to be filled with memories. And as an investor, it's your job to create a space where those memories can be made!

Comparative Market Analysis

If you're an aspiring real estate investor, it's crucial to know about the comparative market analysis (CMA). A CMA is a tool that gives you insights into the prices of similar properties in your area of interest. For example, if you're considering a two-bedroom condo in the city, a CMA will provide data on recent sales or rentals of similar properties in that area.

Why is this important? It helps you gauge the right amount to offer for the property. If the property you're interested in is listed at a much higher price than comparable ones, you might want to rethink your decision. Conversely, if it's listed for a lower price, it could be a great deal, provided you've done your due diligence.

Remember, in real estate, knowledge truly is power. So before making an offer or signing a lease, conduct a CMA to understand what a fair price should be.

Usually, a CMA is conducted by a real estate agent or broker. They identify homes similar to your property of interest, often referred to as *comps*. These comps are evaluated and adjustments are made for differences such as an extra bedroom or a renovated kitchen. Finally, an average price per square foot is calculated to provide an estimated value of the property you're interested in.

As an investor, conducting a CMA is crucial for understanding the market, assessing risk, and estimating potential profit. If the property you're interested in is priced significantly higher than comparable properties, it might be a risky investment. However, knowing the going rate will help you forecast your return on investment if you plan to rent out or resell the property.

You can also conduct a preliminary CMA before engaging a real estate agent. Start by identifying similar properties using online platforms like Zillow or Redfin. Then, compare prices, focusing on the price per square foot. Also, take note of market conditions such as how quickly properties are selling and whether they're selling above or below the asking price. This will give you a sense of the market conditions and help guide your investment decisions.

Projected Returns

Let's take a closer look at how an investor can use the information gathered from a CMA to calculate potential returns and make a profitable investment.

Imagine this scenario: You're considering buying a property with the intention of renting it out. You've done your due diligence, conducted a thorough comparative market analysis, and have a good understanding of the local real estate market. Now, it's time to crunch some numbers and see if this investment could be the one. Here's how to calculate your potential returns:

1. **Estimate the rental income you can expect.** The CMA should give you an idea of what similar properties in the area are renting for. For instance, if similar two-bedroom apartments in the area are renting for $1,500 per month, you could reasonably expect a similar amount.

2. **Tally up your expected expenses.** These will include things like mortgage payments, property taxes, insurance, and maintenance costs. Let's say these amount to $1,200 per month.

3. **Subtract your expenses from your expected rental income to calculate your potential net income.** In this case, you'd be left with $300 each month ($1,500 − $1,200 = $300). This amount would go straight into your piggy bank, contributing to your overall return on investment.

But don't stop there! Consider other factors as well, such as the potential for property value appreciation. If the neighborhood is up-and-coming, your property might significantly increase in value over time, leading to a substantial profit when you decide to sell.

So, if after all this calculation, the rental income comfortably covers your expenses and leaves a decent amount for your savings, then you might just be holding a winning ticket! It means you've found a property that not only pays for itself but also generates income—the dream scenario for any real estate investor.

Just like Max and Edward, equip yourself with the knowledge and be prepared to conquer the real estate market! Remember, every property has a story to tell. Your job is to listen, evaluate, and decide if it's the right one for you. Happy investing!

Conducting a Financial Analysis

It's a big world out there, with opportunities in both residential and commercial properties. But before you jump in, it's important to understand how to analyze your potential investments. This is where key financial metrics come into play. Whether you're looking at an appealing residential property or a sleek commercial building, understanding these numbers can help you make smart, informed decisions. After all, you wouldn't go on a road trip without a map, right? Consider these financial metrics your road map to successful real estate investing!

Return on Investment and Cap Rate

The world of real estate investment is packed with jargon, but two terms are particularly vital to understand: return on investment (ROI) and capitalization rate (cap rate). Think of the ROI as your financial trophy. It's the percentage that tells you how much you've gained or lost relative to your initial investment. In other words, it shows you the bang you're getting for your buck!

Now, the cap rate is a bit different. It's like the heartbeat of an investment property, a vital sign you need to monitor. The cap rate is the ratio of a property's net income (the income after expenses) to its market value. This percentage is a quick way to compare the profitability of different investments. Higher cap rates suggest higher risk but also higher potential returns, and lower cap rates usually indicate lower risk and more stable returns. So, when you're assessing potential investments, remember to check their pulse with the cap rate and visualize your victory lap with the ROI.

Let's say you purchase a condo outright for $200,000 and rent it out, yielding a monthly revenue of $2,000. Your annual income from this property, therefore, is $24,000. After deducting annual expenses such as insurance, taxes, and maintenance, which total $10,000, your net income is $14,000. To calculate your ROI, divide the net income by the total investment and multiply by 100. In this case, it would be ($14,000/$200,000) × 100, which equals a 7% ROI. This means you are earning 7% of your initial investment every year.

Now, imagine another scenario where you purchase a condo for $300,000. You decide to renovate the unit, investing an additional $50,000. So, your total investment is now $350,000. Post-renovation, the condo's value jumps to $400,000. If you choose to sell the condo at this price, your ROI would be (($400,000 − $350,000)/$350,000) × 100, which equals approximately 14.3%. This means you've made a 14.3% return on your investment.

Remember, ROI is your financial scorecard, giving you a clear snapshot of your investment's performance. Whether you're renting out or flipping properties, always analyze your ROI to ensure you're racing toward the finish line in your real estate investment journey.

Now let's turn to real-life examples of cap rate. Imagine you're eyeing an adorable single-family home in an up-and-coming neighborhood. The asking price for the property is $500,000, and after doing your homework, you find out that it can generate an annual net income of $40,000. To calculate the cap rate, you divide the annual net income by the property's value, so in this case, it's $40,000 divided by $500,000, which gives you a cap rate of 8%. That's a strong indication of a profitable investment.

Now, consider a sprawling apartment complex in the city center, with a hefty price tag of $2,000,000. After crunching the numbers, you discover its potential to rake in an annual net income of $100,000. Using the same calculation, this investment offers a cap rate of 5%.

This is lower, indicating a lower return, but also potentially less risk, as this property is in a sought-after location.

These illustrative examples serve to highlight the different cap rates you can encounter in real estate investing. The key takeaway? A higher cap rate often signals a higher potential return, but also higher risk. A lower cap rate, however, could suggest stability and lower risk. Your target cap rate will depend on your individual risk tolerance and investment goals.

Net Operating Income

If you're venturing into commercial real estate, which includes properties like office buildings or retail spaces, you'll need to consider a few more metrics. First is the net operating income (NOI). Think of NOI as the annual profit you pocket after paying all your property's operating expenses but before servicing debt. Let's say, for example, you own a snazzy office building that generates an impressive $500,000 in annual income. From this, you subtract your operating expenses, such as property management, maintenance, and taxes, which total $200,000. Your NOI would be $500,000 − $200,000, leaving you with a healthy $300,000—that's your profit for the year.

Cash-on-Cash Return

Next is the cash-on-cash return. This metric is an absolute gem because it tells you the percentage of your initial investment you'll get back each year as cash flow after all expenses and debt servicing! So if you invest $1,000,000 in a commercial property and after all expenses and mortgage payments, you're left with $75,000 at the end of the year, your cash-on-cash return is ($75,000/$1,000,000) × 100, which gives you a 7.5% return.

Debt Service Coverage Ratio

The debt service coverage ratio (DSCR) tells you if your property's income is enough to cover your mortgage payments. Suppose your

NOI for the year is $125,000 and your total annual mortgage payments are $100,000. Your DSCR would be $125,000/$100,000, giving you a ratio of 1.25. This means you're earning 25% more than you need to pay off your debt, putting you in a comfortable position.

Legal and Regulatory Considerations

Now, strap in and get ready as we venture into the thrilling world of legal and regulatory considerations in real estate investment. This can actually be more exciting than you think. Understanding the law is not just about avoiding trouble; it's also about finding hidden opportunities.

Zoning Laws

Consider this scenario: You've located a nice piece of undeveloped land. It's easy to imagine a large, modern apartment complex standing there. You're already thinking about the potential income it could generate. But before you get too far ahead of yourself, there's an important detail you need to check—the zoning laws.

Zoning laws serve as the guiding principles in real estate development, acting much like a rulebook. They are regulations set forth by local governments that specify how a particular parcel of land can be used. For instance, a piece of land that is zoned as residential might only permit the construction of homes, townhouses, or other types of dwelling units. This means you wouldn't be able to build a commercial structure, such as a shopping mall or office building, on this land. However, land zoned for agricultural use is designated for farming or related activities. This categorization would prohibit the development of structures like a high-rise apartment building. Therefore, understanding zoning laws is critical as they determine the type of development that can occur on a specific plot of land, ensuring that it aligns with the community's planning and development goals.

Think of it like cooking a meal—you wouldn't try to bake a cake in a toaster, right? Similarly, you can't build a skyscraper on land zoned for single-family homes. That beautiful, rustic piece of land you've been eyeing might be zoned for agricultural use only, meaning you could end up with a pumpkin patch instead of multi-family building.

Before you dive into any real estate venture, it's crucial to first investigate the land's zoning classification. This step, which could involve a trip to the city planning department or a visit to the local county website, is a part of your due diligence. Zoning laws, more than just rules, serve as your blueprint. They stipulate what is and isn't possible on a specific piece of land, thereby preventing potential headaches down the line. Seeing them as your guide can help you navigate the complexities of real estate investment. After all, understanding the game's rules is the key to success!

Landlord-Tenant Regulations

The next aspect to consider in the realm of real estate investment is understanding landlord-tenant regulations. Think of these regulations as the rules of engagement in the rental property game, a set of guidelines that govern the relationship between you, the property owner, and your prospective tenants. For instance, imagine you've just purchased a building in the city, complete with several units ready to be rented out. However, it's important to not get too carried away.

Before you start advertising your property and welcoming potential tenants for viewings, it's paramount that you familiarize yourself with the landlord-tenant regulations. These rules cover critical areas that can significantly affect your landlord journey. They include terms for security deposits, outlining how much can be charged and the conditions for return; lease termination, specifying the notice period and the acceptable reasons for ending a lease early; and eviction rules, providing a legal framework for removing a tenant under certain circumstances.

Knowing these regulations inside out will not only help you navigate your journey as a landlord smoothly but also protect you from potential pitfalls and legal disputes. Remember, being a successful landlord isn't just about owning property—it's about understanding your rights and responsibilities within the law.

Professional Legal Advice: Worth Its Weight in Gold

Professional legal advice is often the missing piece of the puzzle in successful real estate ventures. Consider it your secret weapon in navigating the complex maze of property investment. We want you to understand the importance of having an arsenal of lawyers, each specializing in different aspects of real estate, at your fingertips. This team of experts can be instrumental when drafting a lease agreement, negotiating a purchase, or dealing with a difficult tenant.

Having real estate attorneys by your side is invaluable during these times. They not only help you steer clear of potential legal troubles but also provide a sense of security that enables you to focus on what matters most—growing your real estate portfolio.

These professionals are equipped with the expertise to guide you through the intricacies of real estate law, ensuring your transactions are legally sound and your interests protected.

We use multiple lawyers for various situations, thereby minimizing risk and maximizing opportunities. Our approach underscores the significance of professional legal advice in the realm of real estate investment. It's not just about avoiding legal pitfalls; it's about securing peace of mind. And trust us, that peace of mind—knowing we are legally covered while we expand our real estate assets—is truly priceless.

■ ■ ■

This chapter underlines the significance of having a clear why before you venture into the world of real estate. You must have strategic reasons for every property you choose. To make informed decisions, we emphasize thorough research in key areas like market trends, property evaluations, financial metrics, zoning, and legal considerations. This knowledge empowers you to step confidently into the real estate market.

Your journey begins with setting precise goals and evaluating your expertise, time commitment, and risk tolerance. Whether your dream is generating rental income on a beach or flipping properties for profit, this foundation will set you on the path to real estate success.

Chapter 6

Who You Can Trust for Advice

It's time to jump into one of the most key aspects of successful real estate investing—getting advice and finding your mentor. As experienced real estate investors, we've had to figure out when to ask for advice and learn to actually listen to the advice given. We've also had many people reach out to us, asking for help in navigating the complex world of real estate investments.

We understand that starting a new venture can be overwhelming, especially when it involves your hard-earned money and precious time. Finding mentors, asking for advice, and trusting your gut are essential aspects of personal and professional growth—it's all about continuously evolving and expanding ourselves. Asking for advice enables you to tap into the wisdom and experiences of others, providing valuable insights and perspectives that can help you make more informed decisions. Mentors provide guidance, share their wisdom, and help navigate challenges along the way. But more important, trusting your gut enables you to tap into your intuition and make decisions that align with your values and goals.

The tricky part is knowing who the right people are to ask and whether to take their advice. A mentor can be anyone from a successful aunt who has great ideas and knows your personality well or someone who's been in the investment business for ages. Also, figuring out when to listen to their advice or go with your gut feeling is important. In this chapter, we help you figure out how to navigate the world of advice and mentorship. We discuss these topics in-depth and provide real-life examples of how seeking advice and listening to our inner voice has helped us make profitable investments. As experienced investors, we have learned that investing is not just about numbers and financial calculations; it's also about mindset, intuition, and the ability to trust yourself and your instincts. We believe that by understanding the importance of getting advice and finding mentors, you can accelerate your success in real estate investing.

Advice: It's Really Research!

Advice is not just a word; it's a powerful research tool that takes you on a journey of wisdom and experience shared by others. It's like having not just one but hundreds of mentors at your disposal! The collective of experiences, insights, and recommendations of others can be invaluable for making smart, informed decisions, which are essential in real estate investment. And guess what? When you get advice from different people, you might stumble on ideas you never even thought about before. It's like having your own focus group with new and diverse concepts.

So, who should you ask? When you seek advice, you're essentially crowdsourcing information. You're tapping into the knowledge and experiences of many different people, each with their unique perspectives and lessons learned. And the best part? You can ask anyone! From seasoned real estate gurus to your neighbor who also wants to invest in real estate—everyone's experiences can provide a unique piece of the puzzle. The diverse range of experiences that each individual brings to the table can offer a unique and valuable perspective, adding a crucial piece to the puzzle of understanding. By embracing and appreciating the richness of these varied experiences, we all can gain deeper insights and foster a more inclusive and comprehensive understanding of the world around us. So don't be afraid to reach out and seek advice from a diverse group of people; it can only enhance your knowledge and understanding of the market.

Case Study: Networking—The Secret Weapon in Real Estate Investing

Recently, Noelle wanted to sell an investment property in suburban Sussex County, New Jersey. She knew the ins and outs of the industry but faced a challenge: selling her property quickly and without the conventional route of placing it on the multiple listing service. She had put some work into the property, and it was an opportunity to make a profitable sale. Noelle knew she would get a better price for it if she sold before the start of the school year, and it was already toward the end of the summer. But she knew a secret: selling is all about people, connections, and opportunities.

Noelle was on a mission, asking everyone in her network, "Do you know someone who's looking for a starter home in Sussex?" From the people at her dog training class to the patrons of her favorite coffee shop, Noelle tapped into every possible conversation, leaving no stone unturned. Her dedication and pursuit were about to pay off in a massive way.

Eventually, it wasn't anyone in the real estate industry who gave her the lead she needed. A mom-friend from her children's school referred her to a secret weapon: a real estate agent who specialized in starter homes in the exact area of her property. It was like hitting the jackpot. This wasn't just any agent; she had an exclusive list of eager buyers on the hunt for the exact type of house Noelle was selling. Talk about serendipity.

Within three days of showcasing the property, things started to heat up. Not one, but two couples made offers above the asking price! Noelle was absolutely thrilled and accepted the offer of a young couple with two small children. The deal was sealed—she even threw in the trampoline in the backyard. Noelle had not only successfully sold her property but had done so quickly and profitably!

(continued)

Who You Can Trust for Advice

(continued)

> Noelle was not afraid to ask around and ask for advice. It's not always about conventional methods; sometimes, it's about thinking outside the box, taking advantage of opportunities, and leveraging your network. Real estate investing is not just about properties; it's about people, too.

Listen to Your Inner Voice

There comes a time in every investor's journey when you stand at the crossroads of advice and intuition. This point often becomes the defining moment, shaping your journey and carving a unique success path for you.

Listen to your gut!

That's right, your intuition, your gut feeling, your sixth sense, the little angel on your shoulder—whatever you call it—is a powerful ally in your investment journey. At times, it might be the only guide you have when navigating the complex world of real estate investing.

In this uncertain world, even the most seasoned investors can't predict the future with absolute certainty. Market trends ebb and flow, investment strategies evolve, and opportunities arise when least expected. You may have the best mentor, the most competent advice at your fingertips, but remember, no one understands your situation better than you. You are the captain of your ship, the master of your destiny.

Take, for instance, Eric's very own journey. He has had countless instances when he received advice from the top gurus in the industry. They shared their wisdom, yet there are many times he chose to listen to his gut. And guess what? Eric's intuition never disappoints!

We remember an instance when Eric was advised against investing in a property that didn't seem lucrative on the surface. Eric was just starting out and buying his first commercial building. He decided to seek advice from millionaires and successful business people he knew, hoping their success would provide valuable insights on his decision to a purchase particular building he wanted to invest in. He spoke to several different people all with tangible success in business but not specifically in commercial real estate investments. Their responses were unanimous—don't buy the building. They suggested buying stocks instead, or just saving his money for a safer investment, calling this building, in particular, a bad investment.

Despite the discouragement, Eric remained undeterred. He felt strongly that this building would work out for him and saw no reason to let others dissuade him because of his youth or their skepticism. Resolute, he ignored the naysayers and pursued his plan, leading later to a windfall of over $1 million from his first major commercial property acquisition.

Reflecting on this journey, Eric learned two invaluable lessons. The millionaires who had advised against his venture were not professional real estate investors themselves. Although they may have dabbled in property investments and had their fair share of successes and failures, none had made real estate investing their career as he intended to do. Eric's story underscores the importance of seeking advice from those who are well versed in the field one aims to enter.

Another key lesson in Eric's story is his reliance on his gut instinct, especially when dealing with real estate. Although he acknowledges that intuition isn't always reliable all areas of his life, he stresses its infallibility in his property investment decisions.

Eric's journey serves as a powerful reminder that success in real estate investing requires resilience, a strong belief in one's capabilities, and the discernment to seek advice from the right sources. His story is a testament to the power of sticking to your guns and following your instincts in the face of adversity.

Now, we aren't saying that you should disregard professional advice. No, far from it. What we're suggesting is to trust your intuition, listen to your gut when it speaks, especially when it contradicts the popular opinion.

It's your business! It's your life! You have the final say. You are writing your own success story. Your intuition coupled with advice from trusted mentors can work wonders. Your gut feeling can often see beyond the numbers and the trends into the very heart of an investment opportunity.

So, here's our advice to you: *trust your gut!* It's the one companion that will stick with you, guiding you through the highs and lows, navigating the ebbs and flows of the real estate investing journey. Trust your intuition; it's your most potent weapon, your guiding light.

Remember, the most successful investors aren't just those who follow advice. They are the ones who make bold decisions and shape their own destiny! So, be bold, trust your instincts, and carve your unique path in the world of real estate investing!

The Power of Mentorship: Learning from Experts

A mentor is someone who has already walked down the path you're on and can provide guidance and support along the way. They have already experienced both success and failure, learned valuable lessons, and are willing to share their insights with you. Having a mentor can save you time, money, and mistakes by helping you avoid common pitfalls and providing expert advice tailored to your specific needs.

Through the journey of this book, we are your virtual mentors, paving the way for you to navigate the intricate world of real estate investment. Consider us your compass, providing direction based on our wealth of experience and lessons learned from past mistakes. We're here to guide you, ensuring you don't stumble over the same hurdles we did. However, as enthusiastic and committed as we are to your success, it's essential to remember to build a robust support system in real life. There's nothing quite like the tangible support and reassurance from your local community or network that mirror your investment journey. Remember, our wisdom and your real-life connections form a compelling mix, priming you for success in real estate investing.

But how do you find the right mentor? It's essential to seek out someone who aligns with your goals, values, and personality. They should have a proven track record of success, with the experience and knowledge you hope to gain. Don't be afraid to reach out and ask for mentorship—after all, many successful investors are more than happy to share their insights and help others succeed.

And remember, mentorship is not just about receiving advice but also about building meaningful relationships. Your mentor can become a trusted confidant, accountability partner, and lifelong friend, so don't underestimate the power of mentorship in your journey toward real estate success.

Case Study: Find Your Herb

Eric has always been a go-getter. With a fiery ambition and a relentless drive, he began his real estate career hustling his way through the world of residential real estate, climbing up the ladder at an impressive speed. His work ethic and tenacity caught the eye of his firm's owner, a successful woman with a roster of high-end clientele. She saw potential in Eric and gave him an opportunity to work on some of the most prestigious properties in her portfolio. One of these properties belonged to Herb, the man who would become Eric's mentor.

Their first meeting was less than ideal. Eric, young and slightly overconfident, showed up late to an open house. His tardiness did not sit well with Herb, who thought him to be a young and cocky. He gave him a stern dressing-down that left Eric feeling more intimidated than he'd ever felt before. From that moment, Eric made sure to be early for every subsequent meeting, and a friendship began to form between the two men.

Herb ran a successful telemarketing company and invited Eric to see how his business operated. He shared his journey to success, and the two realized they shared a common passion for business. Over the next two years, Herb watched Eric run his business, offering advice and giving him tricks and tips on how to stand his ground.

Then one day, the unexpected happened. Herb proposed they partner on a real estate project. They decided to buy a vacant building that needed $400,000 worth of renovations. Eric was

(continued)

(continued)

ecstatic. He had already done a few renovation projects. Herb, who hated construction, wasn't as sure about jumping head first into renovation, but he trusted Eric implicitly. Together, they experienced the thrill of demolition. Herb even knocked down walls using his own feet. Then they enjoyed the satisfaction of cashing 100% of their money out through refinancing after eight months of hard work.

Fast-forward 23 years, and the bond between Herb and Eric has only strengthened. Their mentorship has evolved into a deep friendship, akin to a father-son relationship. Eric credits his mentor as one of the best things that has happened to him, a testament to the transformative power of mentorship.

Eric's story is a shining example of how a good mentor can accelerate personal and professional growth. It demonstrates that mentorship can come from unexpected places and under unconventional circumstances. It's about finding someone who understands you, makes time for you, and is willing to walk with you on your journey to success.

So how do you find your own Herb?

Not All Mentors Are Created Equal: Choosing the Right Guide for Your Journey

Choosing the right guide for your real estate journey is not a task to be taken lightly. Although asking for advice provides you with varied perspectives and quick insights, mentorship is a long-term commitment, offering you a wealth of experience, personalized guidance, and a solid support system. The difference between the two is much like comparing a compass to a detailed map—both can guide you, but one offers a more comprehensive, step-by-step navigation through your real estate journey.

As the saying goes, "In the multitude of counselors, there is safety." However, it's critical to understand that not all advisors are created equal. Your journey toward real estate success requires strategic guidance from those who have walked the path you're embarking on. Seek out mentors who have experienced what you're trying to accomplish—they'll have the firsthand knowledge, the battle scars, and the wisdom that only comes from weathering the storm.

But how do you ensure the advice you're getting is trustworthy? First, consider their character. It's vital to align with advisors who possess a strong ethical compass, ensuring no conflicts of interest that could compromise your progress. Remember, your success is their success.

In today's digital age, it's easier than ever to vet potential advisors online. Online platforms provide a wealth of information about someone's professional background, experience, successes, and even failures. Look for testimonials, reviews, and records of their past dealings. This will give you a holistic view of their track record, and help you make an informed decision.

Getting to know your potential mentors in a variety of different situations is crucial for building a well-rounded understanding of their persona. Although professional interactions give you a glimpse into their expertise and work ethic, social situations can offer insights into their personality, communication style, and values.

It's important that you like your mentor. Engage with potential mentors in community events, professional seminars, or even casual dinners. It's in these instances where you'll see them in action, observe their interactions, and learn more about their attitudes and philosophies beyond work.

In addition, if the opportunity arises, get to know them and their families. Family situations often bring out a different side of people, revealing elements such as their level of patience, compassion, leadership, and how they deal with challenges.

Real estate investing is as much about relationships as it is about the numbers. Your mentor's ability to balance professional prowess with personal empathy will make a significant difference in your journey. So, broaden your horizons, step out of the boardroom, and get to know your mentor in diverse environments. You're not just choosing a guide; you're choosing a companion for your investment journey.

Finally, we can't say it enough: never underestimate the power of your intuition. That gut feeling can often be an indicator of something that can't be measured or quantified. If something doesn't feel right about your potential mentor, it probably isn't.

Your path to success in real estate investing is your own, unique journey. The right advisors can provide invaluable guidance, but ultimately, the decisions and the victories belong to you. Trust your gut, and embark on this exciting journey with confidence and gusto.

Your Mentor Finder Challenge: Identifying Your Ideal Guide

Finding the right mentor can sometimes feel like trying to find a needle in a haystack. But trust us, it doesn't have to be that way! With a bit of organization and a clear plan, you can turn this into an exciting adventure that leaves you with a pretty good idea of who your perfect mentor should be.

Now, we wouldn't recommend setting up formal job-like interviews with potential mentors—that might be a bit bizarre. But think about it like this: if you were hiring a website developer, you'd want to know about their coding skills and what kind of websites they've created before, right? So why not have a checklist for your future mentor, too? To make things easy, we put together a simple outline that you can use to figure out the must-haves for your mentor. It's almost like creating a shopping list but for a mentor instead!

Remember, being mentored isn't a one-way street. It's not just about what you can learn from them, but also what unique insights you bring to the table. So when you're jotting down your list, think about both what you want to get out of the relationship and what you can add to it. With this approach, you'll be on the right track to finding a mentor who can help you reach your full potential.

Step 1: Determine Your Desired Qualities in a Mentor

Begin by reflecting on your own strengths and weaknesses as a real estate investor. Consider the specific areas where you would benefit from guidance and expertise. Are you looking for mentorship in these areas:

- Market analysis
- Financing strategies
- Negotiation skills
- Property management
- Networking and relationship building
- Confidence
- Street skills

Or something altogether different, not mentioned here? Identifying your areas of need will help you narrow down the type of mentor you're seeking. Jot down at least three of these areas that a mentor can be of help to you. The list can be as long as you need it to be, add more areas if needed. Here's an example:

- Area 1: *Negotiation skills*
- Area 2: *Confidence building*
- Area 3: *Property management*

Step 2: Define Your Mentorship Goals

Next, set clear goals for what you hope to achieve through mentorship. Are you aiming to one of the following:

- Increase your investment knowledge and skills
- Expand your network and connections in the industry
- Receive guidance on specific projects or deals

- Gain insights into overcoming challenges and setbacks
- Have a sounding board to sort through ideas and solutions

Having defined goals will guide your search for the right mentor. Here are three sample goals:

- Goal 1: *Having a confidant in the real estate world*
- Goal 2: *Learning about a specific type of real estate investment*
- Goal 3: *Having someone who can introduce me to other people in the real estate investment world*

Step 3: Look for Potential Mentors

Explore the following avenues to find potential mentors:

- **Real estate investment groups and associations.** Attend local meetings, seminars, and networking events. Engage with experienced investors who may be open to mentorship.
- **Online forums and communities.** Join real estate investment forums, social media groups, and online communities. Participate in discussions and seek out experienced investors willing to mentor.
- **Real estate workshops and seminars.** Attend workshops or seminars hosted by reputable real estate organizations. These events often provide opportunities to connect with established investors.
- **Professional organizations.** Join industry-specific associations related to real estate investing. These groups might offer mentorship programs or facilitate networking with experienced professionals.

In addition to these, jot down other places you will look for a mentor. Here are three examples:

- Location 1: *Local chamber of commerce*

- Location 2: *Colleges or internships*
- Location 3: *Construction projects I am currently involved in*

Step 4: Evaluate Potential Mentors

When evaluating potential mentors, consider the following qualities:

- **Experience and expertise.** Look for mentors with a proven track record of success in real estate investing. They should have a depth of knowledge in the areas you seek guidance.
- **Effective communication.** A mentor should be able to articulate concepts clearly and provide constructive feedback. This fosters a productive learning environment.
- **Patience and empathy.** A good mentor understands the learning curve and is patient in guiding you through challenges. They should be empathetic to your unique situation.
- **Willingness to invest time.** A mentor should be committed to your growth and willing to invest time in your mentorship.
- **Alignment of values and goals.** Ensure that your mentor's values and goals align with your own to maximize the effectiveness of the mentorship.

In addition to these, are there other personal qualities you will look for in a mentor? Here are three examples:

- Quality 1: *Has no agenda*
- Quality 2: *Philanthropic*
- Quality 3: *Strong work ethic*

There you have it! With this simple activity, you now have a clearer picture of who your ideal mentor is, what qualities they should possess, and where you are likely to find them. We can't stress enough that the journey to real estate success is not a solo one; it's a two-way street. Be prepared to contribute, be respectful of their time, and show gratitude for their guidance. The right mentor can provide the winning edge in your quest for real estate greatness! Take your time, trust your instincts, and choose wisely.

■ ■ ■

Consider the information outlined in this chapter as a road map to successfully leveraging others to help achieve your real estate goals. Advice isn't just words, it's like a focus group of different opinions to give you options. And a mentor is just like having a personal expert and pseudo-therapist on your side, guiding you through the twists and turns of real estate.

Cast a wide net when seeking advice. Ask yourself, "Hey, who's got the good stuff?" It's not just the big shots; even your neighbor who's into real estate has something valuable to share. Advice is like building your own dream team of advice-givers. Noelle's story showed us how powerful, and lucrative, casting a wide net and seeking advice can be.

Don't forget to trust your gut. You know those moments when you just feel something's right or wrong? That's like the angel on your shoulder whispering in your ear. Remember Eric's story when all the advice told him not to invest in a property, but his gut said otherwise. And guess who was right? Yes, Eric's gut feeling! He has had loads of moments like that. He's learned to trust his own feelings, even when others have different opinions. It's paid off big time for him and we believe it will for you, too.

And don't forget mentors. They're like your personal coaches in real estate and life. They've been through it all and can guide you like a pro. Eric's mentor, Herb, became like a second dad to him. And they have made millions of dollars together over the years. That's how impactful mentors can be. Mentors are like having a wise guru to help you develop.

All mentors are not created equal. You've got to find someone whose experiences match up with your own journey. Think of it like picking a coach who knows the ins and outs of the game. They might not be making a career out of real estate investing, but their wisdom should still amplify the guidance you're looking for.

But it's not just about what they know, it's also about who they are. You want a mentor with a solid reputation—someone respected in their field. And don't forget the personality factor. You'll want to find someone you vibe with, someone you can easily chat with over a cup of coffee. After all, a great mentorship is as much about connection as it is about learning.

Now it's your turn. Go out there, ask questions, trust yourself, and find your own real estate Jedi master. You've got this!

Chapter 7

Creative Financing

Show Me the Money

If you are reading this book, it is more than likely that you have some notion of what traditional mortgage financing is. Traditional financing is a bit like a well-coordinated dance with four main players: the seller, the buyer, the bank or mortgage lender, and the closing agent. Mastering the dance of mortgage financing is a crucial aspect of real estate investing.

Picture this: You're a buyer, eyeing a gorgeous two-family house offered by a seller. Negotiations have gone well, and now it's time to figure out the money part. You and the seller agree on a price and put it down in a purchase and sale agreement. This document becomes your golden ticket to approach a bank or another mortgage lender to fund the purchase, typically with a bit of your own down payment thrown in. As you secure the funds from the lender, the closing agent takes center stage. Think of closing agents as the choreographers of this dance, guiding the whole process smoothly to its grand finale. They make sure your money finds its way to the seller, and in return, you get a promissory note and a mortgage. Once all is said and done, the seller hands over the deed to the house, and ta-da! You're officially the new owner. The traditional financing dance wraps up on a high note, with everyone playing their parts to perfection.

But here's the twist: to be a savvy real estate investor, you have to know that traditional financing isn't the only song you can or should dance to. In fact, many times it's the last dance you should try. There's an array of creative financing techniques—such as cash-out refinance, seller financing, hard money loans, house hacking, partnerships, and even using your retirement funds—that can diversify and enhance your investment journey. These creative financing methods can unlock new possibilities. Whether you're aiming to seize a deal quickly, navigate around credit issues, or efficiently use your available resources, there's a suitable financing strategy for your needs. Each method has its own rhythm and steps, and mastering them can open up new possibilities for successful real estate investing. So, let's continue to explore these techniques and dance to the beat of our investment goals.

Cash-Out Refinance

Refinance is the most important *R* in the BRRRR Method (buy, rehab, rent, refinance, repeat). Imagine being an investor who owns a rental property. Over the years, you've made substantial improvements, raised rents, and paid down some of the initial mortgage, and now you have a substantial amount of equity built up in this property. At the same time, you've spotted another promising investment opportunity but are short on liquid funds. Enter the world of cash-out refinance.

Let's talk about cash-out refinances in the world of real estate investing. Think of it as uncovering hidden treasure right in your building. This nifty financial move enables you to tap into the equity you've built up in your rental property. Here's the scoop: you essentially borrow more money than you currently owe on your mortgage, use that to pay off the original loan, and then pocket the difference. And guess what? You can use this extra cash to dive into a fresh investment opportunity.

For example, imagine you bought your rental property for $200,000, diligently paid down the mortgage to $100,000 and boosted the property's value by $50,000 through some smart improvements. Thanks to your hard work and a little market appreciation, your property is now valued at a cool $300,000. Now, typically, you can opt for a cash-out refinance for up to 70% of your property's current value, which in this case is $210,000.

So, after settling your original mortgage of $100,000, you'll have a sweet $110,000 left in your hands to invest in a new property. And guess what? You can use the same rental income that you were using before the refinance to make the monthly mortgage payments on that $110,000. It's like turning your property's equity into a springboard for your next investment adventure.

Although a cash-out refinance might seem similar to a home equity loan, it has key differences. A cash-out refinance generally offers more favorable interest terms compared to a traditional home equity loan. Plus, unlike borrowing from a hard money lender or conventional financial institution, the interest on a cash-out refinance is usually tax-deductible.

However, it's important to consider the risks involved. When you opt for a cash-out refinance, your mortgage term gets reset, which means the repayment clock starts all over again. Also, unexpected events, like a sudden drop in rental income, could prove to be a challenge when handling the new monthly payments. But if you're an investor eyeing a lucrative deal and need access to capital quickly, a cash-out refinance can be an effective tool. As always, it's crucial to consult with a financial advisor and weigh the pros and cons before making any major financial decisions.

Seller Financing

You're sitting in one of our investment classes and you hear the teacher mention one of his sellers "holding paper" on his most recent investment. You're intrigued. What could this mean? Welcome to the world of seller financing, a creative method that can change the game for smart real estate investors.

The philosophy behind seller financing, also known as *seller carryback*, is simple yet powerful. The goal is to minimize the use of your own money and instead leverage other people's money. Sounds exciting, doesn't it?

Here's an example of how this works: Suppose you've set your eyes on a perfect rental property. The owner, a retired gentleman, owns the house outright and isn't in a rush to get his hands on a lump sum of cash. Instead, he's more interested in a steady stream of income to supplement his retirement funds. This is where seller financing steps in. Instead of you going to a bank for a mortgage, the seller becomes the bank. He agrees to sell you the property, but instead of getting the full payment upfront, he accepts a nice down-payment to help him move and then regular monthly payments from you until the agreed-on price is paid off. It's a win-win situation: you acquire the property without a traditional mortgage, and the seller enjoys a regular income over an extended period.

The terms of seller financing can vary, but typically the downpayment is lower than traditional mortgages, and interest rates may be negotiable. This can make it an attractive option for investors who might not qualify for conventional financing or don't have a lot of cash on hand.

In seller financing, sellers safeguard their interests through a promissory note and a deed of trust or mortgage. These documents detail the loan terms and give the seller a claim on the property if the buyer defaults. Sellers can foreclose on the property in such a case. They might also require a substantial down payment to reduce the risk of default and thoroughly vet the buyer's financial credentials.

Seller financing can be an appealing option for several reasons. It can expedite the sale process by eliminating the need for buyers to seek traditional bank financing. This method also broadens the pool of potential buyers, including those who might not qualify for conventional loans due to poor credit or nontraditional income sources. Sellers might also be able to command a higher selling price or interest rate, leading to a larger overall return. Instead of a lump sum, sellers receive regular monthly payments, creating a consistent income stream that can be especially beneficial for retirees or investors. Additionally, spreading the receipt of funds over time can offer potential tax benefits by reducing taxable income in a given year. Last, seller financing can reduce some costs associated with selling a property, such as loan origination fees.

Seller financing isn't always an option. It works best with sellers who own their properties free and clear and are open to receiving long-term payments instead of immediate cash. If a seller is under-water on their mortgage or urgently needs a substantial amount of cash, seller financing won't be a viable strategy. But when the stars align and you find a seller open to this arrangement, seller financing can be a game-changer. Especially if you foresee a refinancing opportunity down the line, having seller financing in your real estate investment toolkit can be invaluable.

So, the next time you hear investors talking about "holding papers," you'll know they're discussing the powerful strategy of seller financing. It might not be the right tool for every deal, but when it works, it can unlock incredible opportunities.

Hard Money

Another unique financing option is known as *hard money*. In this scenario, you've just stumbled on a promising property; however, traditional lenders are hesitant to lend to you, perhaps due to your credit score or income verification issues. This is where hard money comes into play.

Hard money is essentially funding from a hard money lending business or an individual specifically for investing in real estate. It's like having a wealthy friend who's ready to back your venture, no questions asked about your income or credit score. This is the first key characteristic of hard money loans—they're far less stringent with their approval requirements compared to traditional lenders.

Now, let's talk about the terms of these loans. Your hard money lender will want their money back sooner rather than later, and they're asking for a higher interest rate. That's pretty much how hard money loans work. They typically have shorter term lengths, higher interest rates, and can often fund a deal within days.

Another interesting aspect of hard money lenders is their expertise in real estate. They're not just moneylenders; they're seasoned real estate professionals. Instead of scrutinizing your credit score or asking for references, they're more interested in your game plan. They'll review your rehab blueprint, your scope of work, and the after-repair value of your investment property to determine loan terms.

However, a word of caution before you dive in: always have your exit strategy ready. Remember, hard money loans are short term. You don't want to find yourself in a position where your loan runs out before your project is complete. So, plan ahead, strategize, and use hard money wisely to maximize your real estate investments.

House Hacking

House hacking is a strategy we often recommend, especially for young investors who have the freedom to try out unconventional living arrangements. If you're not tied down with family responsibilities or the need for a permanent home, this can be an incredible opportunity to kickstart your real estate journey. We highly endorse it, particularly for younger investors who can explore nontraditional living situations.

House hacking is all about savvy investing, and it can be a real game-changer, especially if you're new to the real estate world. Picture yourself buying a two-, three-, or even a four-family home. You move into one of the units and rent out the others. The rent from your tenants helps pay off your mortgage. That's the essence of house hacking in a nutshell.

This strategy comes with several perks. First, you put your property to work right away. Instead of waiting for years to see a return on your investment, you start seeing it as rental income. Plus, it can make homeownership way more affordable than renting, which is a win-win!

Now, don't get us wrong, being a landlord can have its challenges. You'll need to handle tenant issues, manage maintenance, and deal with all the ins and outs of property management. But at the end of the day, it's like getting a hands-on, real-world crash course in real estate investing!

Here's an important point: house hacking is all about thinking creatively and breaking out of the traditional homeownership mold. It's the kind of strategy that says, "If there's a will, there's a way." If you're up for the challenge, house hacking can be your ticket to becoming a seasoned real estate investor.

Did you know that the Federal Housing Administration (FHA) offers loans that are perfect for house hackers? With an FHA loan, you can buy a property with as little as 3.5% down, and, yes, multiunit properties are fair game. With an FHA loan, you can purchase up to a four-family home. The only catch is that you must live in it as your primary home for a predetermined amount of time. That means you could potentially buy a duplex, live in one unit, rent out the other, and only put down a fraction of the upfront cost. It's like the universe is saying, "Go ahead, give house hacking a shot!"

Partnering Up

Although the thought of sharing your maiden real estate venture with another individual or group may initially appear intimidating, it's important to understand that partnerships can be both strategic and beneficial, particularly when you're just setting foot in the industry. Teaming up with other investors can significantly expand your capabilities and resources. However, it's crucial to choose your partners carefully and establish clear guidelines from the get-go.

When we talk about partnerships, we're not just discussing the division of costs and risks. We're also referring to gaining access to a partner's resources, which can encompass their financial ability, expert knowledge, or expansive network. This is all about leveraging each other's strengths to achieve mutual objectives. As the saying goes, "two heads are often better than one." In the context of real estate investing, this collaboration could equate to a wealth of knowledge, additional people power, and access to a wider range of financing options.

However, like all strategies, partnerships come with their own set of advantages and disadvantages. On the plus side, partnering can provide added financial strength, shared risk, and a broader skill set. It enables you to pool resources and expertise, making larger or more complex investments possible. Moreover, a good partner can complement your skills, fill gaps in your knowledge, and provide moral support.

On the downside, partnerships also require compromise and can lead to potential conflicts. Differences in opinion about investment strategies, management styles, or exit plans can create tension. Furthermore, you're financially tied to your partner, so if they face financial difficulties, it could affect the partnership and the investment.

Before embarking on a partnership, it is important to consider these key elements:

- **Choosing the right partner is crucial.** This person or group should align with your investment vision and strategies, and there must be mutual trust and respect. Remember, a partnership is not a temporary arrangement—you're initiating a journey together.

- **Once you've identified a potential partner, you must set clear guidelines.** These should include defining roles, responsibilities, and how profits or losses will be divided. Transparency and open communication are vital here. They not only help prevent future conflicts but also pave the way for a smooth and successful partnership.

If you're considering venturing into real estate investing but are apprehensive about the financial commitment, remember that partnerships can be a viable option. With the right partner, your aspiration of becoming a real estate investor can become a reality. So, take the leap and explore the world of real estate partnerships, which could serve as your springboard to success in real estate investing.

Dipping into Your Retirement

Using your retirement funds to invest in real estate is a strategy that can potentially be a game-changer for your financial future. It's worth noting that for some people, their real estate investments serve as the cornerstone of their retirement nest egg. However, it's equally crucial to understand the rules and risks associated with this approach.

One intriguing avenue to explore is the self-directed Individual Retirement Account (IRA). This specialized type of IRA enables you to broaden your investment horizons, and real estate stands as one of the prime opportunities. But, and it's a substantial *but*, the IRS closely monitors this field. They've established strict guidelines to ensure a level playing field. For instance, you can't transform your real estate investment into your personal residence; it's strictly a hands-off arrangement. Additionally, all financial transactions related to the property must flow through your IRA, under the watchful eye of the financial referee.

Another option is borrowing from your 401(k) to access funds for your real estate venture. Although this might seem like a tempting shortcut, it comes with a big "proceed with caution" sign. Failing to repay the loan can categorize it as an early distribution, which can trigger taxes and early withdrawal penalties—not a play you want in your financial playbook.

One crucial point to consider is the long-term impact of prematurely tapping into your retirement funds. The magic of compound interest is what powers the growth of your retirement savings over time. By withdrawing money before reaching retirement age, you risk disrupting that magic, potentially leaving you with a smaller nest egg in the end.

Before making any moves, a consultation with a financial advisor is non-negotiable. These seasoned coaches can help you understand the potential risks and rewards, all tailored to your unique financial situation. They'll develop a game plan that aligns with your financial goals, ensuring that real estate becomes a strategic play in your retirement playbook.

Although the allure of real estate investment is undeniable, it's essential to proceed with caution, respecting the rules and crafting a well-thought-out strategy. For many, real estate investments serve as the foundation of their retirement nest egg. So, play the game wisely, and let your real estate investments work toward securing your financial future.

■ ■ ■

You've come a long way in our book so far, and like most people, you have a grasp of traditional mortgage financing and its crucial role in real estate investing. It's a process that involves the seller, the buyer, the bank or mortgage lender, and the closing agent. When all the pieces fall into place, you end up as the proud owner of your chosen property.

But here's something to remember: traditional financing isn't your only option in real estate investing. From unlocking your property's equity through cash-out refinancing to exploring seller financing, securing hard money loans for fixer-uppers, or the innovative tactic of house hacking, you have numerous options to choose from. Also, using your retirement funds for real estate investments can be a game-changer, but it demands careful planning and strict adherence to IRS regulations.

Each of the financing methods we explored in this chapter has its own unique features, and mastering them can open up new avenues for success in real estate investing. As you continue on your journey, we encourage you to explore these techniques, adapt them to your investment goals, and pave your own path toward financial success. The world of real estate is always evolving, and with the right financing strategies, you can stay ahead of the curve.

Chapter 8

Building Your Team

When diving into real estate investing, your team is your rock. Think of your team as a winning football squad—everyone has a crucial role. Your team may include experts like real estate agents, attorneys, accountants, contractors, and more. The right team lightens your load and adds invaluable insights. They help you navigate the complex real estate world and make sound, goal-aligned decisions. But it's not just about hiring pros; it's about finding those who share your vision, fostering open communication, and nurturing a respectful, collaborative environment.

The key to building a good team is identifying who you need and understanding their roles. Real estate investment is not a solo sport. It's a team game. And the stronger your team, the higher your chances of scoring big in real estate. So, let's get started on building your dream team!

Your Real Estate Investment Team: The People in Your Neighborhood

Just as the old *Sesame Street* tune asks, "Who are the people in your neighborhood?," when it comes to real estate investing, you're going to need a neighborhood of your own—a neighborhood of experts, that is. These are the people you're going to rely on, work with, and learn from. They're the ones who will help you build your real estate empire.

Think about your neighborhood. It's full of different people, each with their unique roles, right? Similarly, your real estate investment team should have varied professionals, each playing a specific role.

Let's go down the street of your investment neighborhood and meet each of these professionals:

- **The lawyer.** You'll want a real estate savvy lawyer in your corner. They ensure all contracts are legally binding and protect your interests during deals. When challenges arise, they're the people offering sage advice and legal strategies.

- **The contractor.** Your contractor is your go-to for all things construction-related. They assess properties, provide estimates, and oversee renovations. They keep you from buying what might seem like a bargain but is actually a money pit.

- **The architect.** Need to revamp a purchased property? Your architect can transform an outdated layout into a lucrative living space. They help you visualize possibilities and deliver plans that comply with local building codes.

- **Administrative people.** Administrative staff keep your operations running smoothly. They handle paperwork, coordinate appointments, and manage day-to-day tasks. They're the glue keeping your team together.

- **The financial planner.** Your planner helps you understand the financial implications of your real estate investments. They can project future trends, plan for taxes, and help you set and achieve financial goals.

- **The accountant.** Your accountant handles the numbers. They manage your books, ensure tax compliance, and provide financial reports. They're instrumental in making sure your earned revenue ends up in your pocket and not the IRS's.

- **The real estate agent.** Your agent knows the local market inside and out. They help you find properties, negotiate deals, and understand local real estate trends. They're your eyes and ears on the ground.

- **The mortgage broker or bank for lending.** Unless you're sitting on a pile of cash, you'll need a reliable lender. They provide the funds you need to purchase properties and can help navigate the complex loan process.

- **The insurance agent.** Your insurance agent is there to safe-guard your investments. They understand the various risks associated with real estate and can guide you to the right poli-cies to protect your assets.

- **The appraiser.** An appraiser provides an objective, unbiased valuation of a property. Their appraisals are critical when secur-ing financing or setting a selling price.

- **The go-to title company.** Your title company ensures the property title is legitimate, so you don't buy a property only to find out someone else can lay claim to it. They also handle the nitty-gritty of closing.

Remember, you're not just building a team; you're creating your own neighborhood of professionals. The right team can make the difference between a profitable investment and a costly mistake, so choose your neighbors wisely. Make sure they not only have the expertise you need but also share your vision and commitment to success.

Diversity Is Key

Venturing into the dynamic universe of real estate investment reveals a pivotal truth: a diverse team is not just an advantage—it's an abso-lute necessity. As we've charted our course through the complex waters of this industry, we've discovered that an effective team is not simply multiple individuals working together; it's a multifaceted entity formed by professionals each possessing unique expertise.

Visualize your team as a sophisticated machine, each part per-forming its specific role. When all parts operate in sync, the machine functions at its optimal capacity. Similarly, your real estate investment team should be composed of experts, each specializing in different areas. In numerous situations, it's beneficial to have a network of professionals in each specific field that you can rely on. This doesn't just mean having one go-to person per area of expertise. Instead, you really should have multiple contacts in each field whom you can reach out to when needed.

Consider having a duo of real estate agents on your team. One could be a specialist in residential properties, and the other might excel in commercial real estate. This combination ensures you're prepared to seize various investment opportunities that come your way.

Likewise, having more than one contractor on your team can be beneficial, especially if each one specializes in a different area. One contractor could be a renovation and remodeling guru, and another might excel in new construction. This breadth of skills enables you to effectively handle a wide array of projects.

Diversity in your legal representation is of paramount importance, especially when it comes to real estate. The field of law is vast and multifaceted, and having a diverse team of legal professionals can significantly enhance your ability to navigate the complex landscape of real estate law. For instance, you might benefit from having a lawyer who is an expert in contract law. They can help you understand the intricacies of purchase agreements and contracts, ensuring that your interests are protected during transactions. This expertise is invaluable in avoiding potential pitfalls and ensuring smooth property transactions.

Concurrently, it could be beneficial to have another lawyer on your team who specializes in property law. Their knowledge can guide you through the nuances of zoning laws and property disputes, offering insights that could save you time and money in the long run. They can also help ensure you're adhering to all relevant regulations and laws pertaining to property ownership.

You get the message: having multiple members in certain roles can prove practical. For example, if one of your contractors is unavailable due to unforeseen circumstances or other commitments, having a backup contractor ensures your projects continue without interruption.

We both have multiple experts at our disposal whom we can rely on in any particular situation. Building a diverse team of professionals with varied specializations not only prepares you to handle a wide range of situations but also provides you with a wealth of knowledge and perspectives. It's akin to having a multi-tool at your disposal, ready and equipped to tackle any challenge that comes your way in your real estate investment journey.

Case Study: The Power of a Diverse Team and Substitutions

Judith was a real estate investor with a varied and diverse team. She had always believed in the power of multiple options and, thus, had intentionally built a network of vendors who performed the same job function. This strategy enabled her to mix and match based on each project's unique needs, and it really paid off during one particular real estate transaction.

It all began when Judith set her sights on an old, derelict apartment building in a rapidly gentrifying neighborhood. She, as most real estate investors, had an eye for seeing potential where others saw decay. Her plan was to purchase the building, renovate it, and transform it into rental apartments, capitalizing on the increasing rental demand in the area.

Right from the start, Judith knew that this undertaking would require extensive renovation work. She reached out to her favorite contractor, Miguel, who specialized in remodeling older properties. However, just as they were about to kick off the project, Miguel suffered a serious injury in an unrelated job, making him unavailable for several weeks.

This could have been a major setback, but Judith's network came to her rescue. She had another contractor, Todd, whom she'd worked with on smaller projects in the past. Todd primarily dealt with new construction but was eager to expand his portfolio. With Miguel out of commission, Judith brought Todd onboard.

Meanwhile, Judith was also negotiating the financing for the project. Her usual mortgage broker had proposed a traditional loan structure, but the terms weren't as favorable as she'd hoped. But as always, Judith had options; she decided to reach out to another broker she'd met at a networking event. This broker specialized in hard money loans.

(continued)

(continued)

The new broker managed to secure a hard money loan with terms that were far more suitable for Judith's project. The loan offered quicker access to funds, enabling Judith to expedite the renovation process and get the apartments to market sooner.

In the end, Judith's diverse network saved her from what could have been a disastrous situation. Her ability to mix and match vendors based on her immediate needs enabled her to navigate the challenges that came her way. The project was not only completed on time but also exceeded her initial expectations in terms of both aesthetics and financial return.

Just remember that reaching out to different professionals doesn't mean you're being disloyal. Sure, we all have our go-to people because we've built strong relationships with them. But at the end of the day, you're an investor, right? Your main focus should be on getting the job done the way you want it, so don't hesitate to work with whoever can deliver the best results for you. It's all part of the game!

How to Assemble Your Team

Building a solid team in real estate investing is vital because they are the ones responsible for turning your property investment ideas into reality. A dependable team not only adds value to your properties but also helps you minimize potential risks, making your real estate investment journey smoother and more profitable in the long run.

First and foremost, you should never underestimate the power of referrals. During our careers, we've found that some of the most proficient professionals we've worked with came to us through recommendations from trusted contacts. So, whether it's friends, family, or colleagues, don't hesitate to ask if they know of any real estate professionals who would be a good fit for your team. You might be surprised at the gems you can uncover through this method.

Networking is another crucial strategy. It's not just about trading business cards, it's about building relationships and having meaningful conversations. You could meet potential team members anywhere—community events, business gatherings, or even casual social settings. The trick is to stay alert and grab opportunities.

Conferences are a treasure trove for meeting industry pros—agents, lawyers, contractors, lenders, you name it. Try to attend these events when you can. You'll gain insights and might even bump into potential team members. And if you decide to become a real estate agent, don't forget about industry associations like the National Association of Realtors. By joining, you get access to resources and connect with other members. Similarly, real estate investment clubs, both local and online, are great places to find like-minded professionals.

In the digital era, real estate social media groups have become an indispensable tool. Platforms like LinkedIn and Facebook host numerous groups where investors and industry professionals interact. These groups are not just for discussion; they're a platform for building relationships and discovering potential team members.

Then there's the power of online research. A simple Google search can lead you to local professionals in your area. Take your time to check out their websites, read their reviews, and explore their portfolios. This step enables you to get a sense of their expertise, past projects, and the quality of their work. Additionally, you can often find valuable insights about their reputation and reliability from other clients' experiences, helping you make more informed decisions when assembling your team for your real estate ventures.

Last, always keep an eye on the world around you. If you come across a property that impresses you or a deal that was handled exceptionally well, don't hesitate to ask about the professionals involved. These individuals have proven their worth, and they could be a fantastic addition to your team.

■ ■ ■

Building a strong team is a process that requires time, patience, and a lot of networking. This team doesn't just lighten your workload;

they also provide diverse views and insights that can make your journey less stressful and more lucrative. They assist you in navigating the complex world of real estate from transactions and regulations to market trends. They're there to guide you toward informed decisions that align with your investment goals. Once you have the right people by your side, your journey into real estate will become much smoother and more rewarding.

Chapter 9

Taking Control of Your Transactions

Entering the world of real estate investing is thrilling, definitely lucrative, and not exactly easy. Real estate investing is about making smart decisions, having a well-thought-out plan, and most importantly, being in the driver's seat. We've been around the block in real estate investing and we can tell you this: mastering the art of control over your transactions is key to a thriving and long-lasting career.

The real estate market is always changing, and being in control doesn't mean just reacting to these changes. Being in control of your real estate transactions is about setting clear goals, crafting a robust business plan, staying ahead of the curve, assembling a dependable team, and keeping a tight grip on your finances. When you're in control, you're not leaving your success to chance or market fluctuations. You're steering your business toward a prosperous future.

And this sense of control isn't just about your overall business. This control should be evident in every single transaction you make. From getting the legal details right to doing your homework thoroughly before each deal, every step demands your focus and careful management. And guess what? There's new technology being developed every day that can help you maintain meticulous records, negotiate like a pro, and navigate each transaction with ease.

Being in control of your transactions and overall business isn't a one-time thing. You must constantly revisit your strategies, build solid relationships, and never stop learning. Control is about embracing the latest tech, prioritizing your customers' happiness, and caring about your reputation. These are your secret weapons in maintaining control amidst changes and uncertainties.

Be an Active Participant

Real estate investing isn't a "set it and forget it" endeavor. Each transaction calls for ongoing attention and active engagement. Here's why favoring an active approach outshines a passive one.

Knowing your market is crucial. Markets are like the weather—always changing, influenced by everything from big economic trends to local events. When you're an active investor, you're keeping tabs on these changes. This enables you to make decisions at the right time to either bump up your profits or soften the blow of potential losses. However, if you're leaning back and taking a passive role, chances are you'll miss these opportunities or find it tough to respond quickly to market downturns.

Every transaction has its own set of potential hiccups—legal issues, unexpected property repairs, you name it. But here's the thing: when you're actively engaged, you're more likely to spot these challenges early because you're right there in the thick of things. This means you can take steps to tackle these problems head-on, saving yourself from financial headaches down the line.

Also, being active in your management helps you build strong relationships with everyone involved in a transaction—think real estate agents, tenants, contractors, legal experts. Keeping the lines of communication open and responding promptly builds trust and reliability, leading to better deals, smoother transactions, and long-lasting partnerships. When you're hands-on in managing your transactions, every deal becomes a learning experience. You'll pick up insights and lessons that can help you fine-tune your strategies, up your negotiation game, and deepen your understanding of the market.

While taking a back seat in investment might seem like less work, it's active management that really unlocks the potential of your real estate investments. Being an active participant keeps you in tune with market movements, helps you dodge risks, strengthens relationships, and promotes constant learning—all contributing to more successful transactions. So, for any budding real estate investor, our advice is clear: step up, take charge, and be an active participant in your transactions.

Be the Chief Cook and Bottle Washer—CEO and the Intern All in One

Are you familiar with the phrase, "chief cook and bottle washer"? It means that your responsibilities include absolutely everything, from the highest level (chief cook) to the lowest (bottle washer). The role of a chief cook and bottle washer in the world of real estate investing is a crucial one. It's the person who has their hands in every aspect of the business, from the initial property search to the final sale or rental. And trust us, this level of involvement isn't about micromanaging. It's about knowing every nut and bolt of your business, which in turn drives confident decision-making. Imagine if you could spot potential issues before they become problems or identify hidden opportunities that others might overlook. That's the power of being a chief cook and bottle washer.

But how do you get there? You must start with a hunger for knowledge and understanding. Dive headfirst into learning about every aspect of the industry. This doesn't mean you need to become an expert in everything, but you do need to understand the landscape. We like to say, it means knowing just enough to be dangerous. This includes areas such as property valuation, real estate law, financing options, and construction processes. And let's not forget the importance of understanding the local real estate market, including demographic trends and future development plans.

Now, you may be asking, "Eric, Noelle, where do I start?" Start where you're most comfortable and gradually expand your knowledge base. There are plenty of resources out there—online courses, real estate books, podcasts, and industry events. Remember the BRRRR strategy we talked about? This is the perfect framework to guide your learning journey. Each letter represents a key area of real estate investing—buying, rehabbing, renting, refinancing, and repeating. By breaking down the process, you can tackle each step one at a time.

But the learning doesn't stop there. As a chief cook and bottle washer, you've got to keep your finger on the pulse of the market, staying tuned to the latest news, trends, and tech. You need to be agile, ready to adapt your strategies based on market dynamics. And don't underestimate the power of networking. Building relationships with other real estate investors, brokers, and industry experts can provide valuable insights and opportunities.

Done right, being a chief cook and bottle washer empowers you to spot the right deals, negotiate effectively, and steer your real estate business toward success. Yes, it demands time, effort, and a never-stop-learning attitude. But remember, every bit of knowledge you gain, every relationship you nurture, and every decision you make with confidence contributes to your control over your transactions.

Managing Your Team and Yourself

So, you've got your team together, and you're all set to dive into the world of real estate investing. That's fantastic! But here's a nugget of wisdom: staying on top of things is crucial. It's like being the conductor of an orchestra—you've got to ensure every instrument is in tune and playing in harmony.

Think about it. Real estate transactions can be complex beasts. They involve a ton of moving parts, from legal paperwork to financial calculations, market analyses, and negotiations. Even the most simple transaction can feel a bit like spinning plates, right? But that's where being on top of things comes in. You must keep an eye on each of these elements, ensuring nothing slips through the cracks.

And it's not just about the deals themselves. You must also know about leading your team effectively. Each member has their own role to play, their own tasks to handle. As the leader, it's your job to ensure everyone knows what they're doing, stays motivated, and works together smoothly. Regular check-ins, clear communication, and a bit of team spirit can go a long way.

Don't forget about yourself in all this. Managing your own tasks and responsibilities is just as important. This could mean anything from staying updated on market trends, networking with industry professionals, or continuing your professional development. Remember, a great leader isn't just someone who manages others well—they also know how to manage themselves.

Staying on top of your real estate investment deals might seem like a lot, but trust us—it's this attention to detail and proactive management that can make the difference between a good deal and a great one.

Managing a real estate investment team isn't always a walk in the park, but these four best practices can make things feel a bit smoother:

- **Communication is key.** Make sure you're keeping open lines of communication with your team. Regular meetings, whether in-person or virtual, can ensure everyone's on the same page and any issues are addressed promptly.

- **Set clear expectations.** It's essential that each team member knows their role and what's expected of them. Clarity can prevent misunderstandings and keep your team working efficiently toward common goals.

- **Regularly review and assess work.** It's important to regularly check on the quality and progress of your team's work. This doesn't mean micromanaging, but rather ensuring that standards are being met and projects are on track. Constructive feedback is crucial here—it can help your team members improve, learn, and grow. Plus, it shows you're actively involved and care about the work being done. Remember, continuous improvement can lead to success in the ever-evolving real estate market.

- **Recognize and reward effort.** A little appreciation goes a long way. Recognizing your team members' hard work and rewarding them can boost morale and motivate them to continue doing their best.

Remember, a well-managed team can be your greatest asset in real estate investment. So, invest your time and effort in nurturing it.

A Day in the Life of a Real Estate Investor

It's essential to remember that every investor's routine can vary greatly, but we can provide a general overview based on our personal experiences and those of our students, partners, and colleagues.

Morning Start

The workday for most real estate investors often kicks off bright and early, typically about 7 a.m. The morning is usually dedicated to catching up on the latest happenings in the market. This might involve scanning local news for any events that might have a bearing on specific properties. Additionally, the early hours are a great time to sift through and respond to any pending emails from the previous day.

Once you've got a handle on the current market landscape and cleared your inbox, it's time to dive into the heart of the business—the ongoing deals. You might find yourself reviewing contracts, negotiating terms with sellers or buyers, or even meeting with real estate agents to discuss potential opportunities. If you're managing properties that are currently under renovation, scheduling a site visit might be on your to-do list.

Remember to start your day with clear intentions. Knowing your top priorities and long-term goals from the outset will guide you throughout your day and keep you focused. Imagine setting out on a journey without a destination; you'll end up going around in circles. It's the same with your investment career—have your end goal in mind.

Midday Action

As midday rolls around, it's often time for meetings with prospective clients or partners. Networking plays a pivotal role in real estate investing, so lunch or coffee meetups are commonplace. These gatherings also serve as an excellent opportunity to touch base with legal advisors or financial consultants to delve into the finer details of specific deals.

Afternoon Admin

The afternoon typically sees more administrative tasks. This might involve filing paperwork, responding to additional emails, or ensuring that all financial matters are squared away. For investors who manage rental properties, part of the afternoon might be allocated to resolving any tenant-related issues. This is also a time when an investor may spend time researching future deals, driving for dollars, or contacting potential leads.

Evening Wrap-Up

As the day starts to wrap up, it's a great time to take a step back and think strategically. This is when an investor can have a good hard look at their portfolio, evaluate how their current game plan is working, and start laying out their next steps. It's also a pretty sweet spot for some professional growth—maybe join in on a webinar or dive into some reading to sharpen those investment strategies. Plus, jotting down what needs to be done the next day makes sure nothing from today gets forgotten. The goal is staying organized and having a clear picture of what's coming up next. This way, you're ready to tackle tomorrow head-on.

Remember, this is just a general blueprint. Each investor will have a unique daily routine depending on their specific investments and their personal approach to the business. However, one constant remains: successful real estate investing hinges on active participation, continuous learning, and meticulous planning.

Best Practices of an Organized Investor

We firmly believe that organization is the cornerstone of success in this ever-evolving field. The real estate market is fluid and fast-paced, with numerous moving parts that require attention. Thus, having a well-structured approach to your day-to-day operations can significantly enhance your productivity and effectiveness.

Maintain a Strong Daily Schedule

Developing a strong daily schedule is not just about organizing your time; it's about creating a strategic road map for your day. By allocating specific time blocks for different tasks, such as prospecting, property inspections, meetings with vendors, and administrative work, you ensure that every activity has its place, and nothing gets overlooked.

Case Study: The Power of Routine

We know a successful investor, Samuel, in New York City. Sam is driven by his routine. His secret weapon is his daily schedule, where he allocates specific time blocks for every task, including prospecting new properties, property inspections, meetings with vendors, and administrative work. This disciplined approach ensures that no task was ever overlooked.

A couple of years ago, Sam came across a promising investment opportunity—an apartment complex in Brooklyn. There was fierce competition for this project, and Sam had to move quickly if he wanted to bid on it. Some competing investors were quick to make offers, but Sam stuck to his organized routine. He set aside time to inspect the property thoroughly, review all legal documents, assess renovation costs, and calculate potential returns.

During this process, Samuel discovered several red flags. The building's plumbing system was severely outdated and would require a costly upgrade. Furthermore, the property was located in a flood zone, which would result in higher insurance premiums and potential risk. Through his extensive research, he also learned about upcoming zoning changes in the area that could potentially devalue the property. He decided to pass on the opportunity.

Another investor who had been enticed by the property's potential returns and location overlooked these issues.

(continued)

(continued)

They didn't allocate enough time to carry out their due diligence and hastily jumped into the deal. As a result, they faced substantial renovation costs, high insurance premiums, and decreasing property values.

Sam had a routine that he knew worked. His commitment to organization and thorough research saved him from this predicament. His detailed approach enabled him to uncover risks that others missed, demonstrating the value of careful planning and organization in real estate investment. Sam knew successful investing is not just about finding the right opportunities but also about effectively identifying and avoiding the wrong ones.

Having a well-structured schedule enables you to manage your time effectively. Instead of jumping from one task to another haphazardly, a schedule provides a clear plan for anything you do. Each task gets a dedicated slot, which helps prevent multitasking and reduces the risk of tasks falling through the cracks. This way, you can give each task your undivided attention, enhancing the quality of your work.

Just keep in mind, it's important to roll with the punches when it comes to your schedule. Sometimes, stuff pops up out of nowhere— could be a problem or maybe even a golden opportunity. You might need to shuffle things around a bit to accommodate these surprises. But if you've got a solid schedule to start with, one that gives you a good structure, it makes it way easier to adapt on the fly when you need to.

Use Technology to Simplify and Automate Tasks

In our modern, digital age, technology serves as a powerful tool in the realm of real estate investment. Embracing software and apps can revolutionize how you navigate your day-to-day operations, making processes more efficient and effective.

One of the significant advantages of these technological tools is their ability to streamline property tracking. Instead of sifting through piles of paperwork or numerous spreadsheets, management software can consolidate all your property-related information into one accessible platform. This includes everything from property details and tenant information to maintenance schedules and providing a comprehensive overview immediately.

Managing finances is another area where these digital solutions shine. They simplify financial tracking by automating income and expense recording. You can easily monitor payments from tenants and contractors, eliminating the risk of human error that comes with manual data entry. In addition, these tools can generate detailed financial reports, giving you valuable insights into your investment performance.

And don't forget that simple tools like calendar and task management apps can transform your phone into a personal assistant. Calendar apps help you manage time efficiently by scheduling appointments and setting reminders. Task management apps let you track tasks, create to-do lists, and prioritize work. Integrated with other software, these tools enhance organization and time management in your real estate investment activities.

We love texting! Being able to text and remain accessible can seriously be a game-changer for your dealings. Messaging can be the key difference in customer interactions, whether it's wrapping up transactions or setting up appointments. Plus, unlike phone calls, texts give you a written record of what's been said—pretty useful, right? But remember to keep your communication on point and efficient, and don't let it mess with your organization.

Just remember, it's all about finding the tech that fits you like a glove. The world of technology is always zooming forward. So, make sure you're staying in the loop about fresh websites or apps that can help automate your business. They can take some of those pesky tasks off your hands, simplifying your life and freeing up your time. This way, you get to focus more on the strategic stuff, which is where the real magic happens!

Delegate, Delegate, Delegate!

Understanding that you're not alone in your venture is crucial. Delegating responsibilities to your team members based on their strengths and expertise can be a game-changer for your business.

Delegation is more than just a tool to lighten your workload; it empowers your team members and fosters a sense of trust and responsibility. When tasks are assigned according to individual strengths and areas of expertise, team members can excel in their roles, leading to higher productivity and efficiency. It also encourages professional growth as they gain experience and confidence in their abilities.

Moreover, delegation enables you to free up valuable time that can be better spent on strategic decisions. As a real estate investor, your role involves making high-level decisions that can significantly affect the future of your investments. These could range from deciding which properties to invest in and determining renovation budgets to crafting long-term investment strategies.

By delegating routine tasks or those outside your area of expertise, you can focus on these critical decisions without getting overwhelmed by day-to-day operations. Plus, it provides an opportunity for you to see the bigger picture and plan for the future, ensuring the sustainable growth of your real estate portfolio. Just remember: trust but verify. Delegation is a great tool, but at the end of the day, this is your project, and you are ultimately responsible for your business.

Foster Clear and Open Communication

Clear and open communication forms the backbone of any successful business relationship, including those in real estate investment. This involves regularly updating your vendors, contractors, and employees; providing feedback; and ensuring everyone is aligned with your objectives. Concurrently, nurturing strong relationships with key players, assessing their performance, and maintaining high standards are equally vital.

Consider each interaction with your vendors, contractors, and employees as an opportunity to reinforce your objectives and expectations. Regular updates not only keep them informed about the status of projects but also make them feel valued and involved. This approach fosters a collaborative environment where everyone is working toward the same goal.

Providing feedback, both positive and constructive, is an essential part of this communication process. Praise can reinforce good practices and boost morale, while constructive criticism can help address issues and improve performance. Remember, feedback should be clear, specific, and framed in a way that encourages improvement rather than causing defensiveness.

However, listening is just as important in maintaining open communication. Encourage your vendors, contractors, and employees to share their ideas, concerns, or challenges. Their on-the-ground insights can provide valuable perspectives that can help in decision-making and problem-solving.

Nurturing strong relationships with your vendors and contractors is crucial because they are integral to your investment operations. Regularly assess their performance to ensure they are meeting your expectations and delivering quality work. This could involve reviewing their work, checking adherence to timelines, and assessing the value they bring to your projects.

By keeping everyone updated, providing feedback, assessing performance, negotiating fair contracts, and maintaining high standards, you can create a collaborative and efficient operation aligned with your investment objectives.

Keep Meticulous Records

Keeping meticulous records of your financial transactions, including income, expenses, and investment performance, is a fundamental practice in real estate investment that should not be overlooked. This practice plays a vital role in guiding your decision-making process, ensuring tax compliance, and providing an accurate picture of your investment's health.

Keeping detailed financial records provides valuable insights into the profitability and performance of your investments. By tracking income such as rent payments and expenses such as mortgage payments, property taxes, and maintenance costs, you can calculate the net income from your properties. Meanwhile, recording investment performance, like appreciation or depreciation over time, can help you assess whether your investment strategy is working or if adjustments are needed.

These records guide your decision-making process. With a clear understanding of your financial situation, you can make informed decisions about future investments, such as whether to buy more properties, sell existing ones, or perhaps invest in property improvements to increase rental income. It can also help you identify patterns or trends, such as seasonal fluctuations in rental income, which can inform your budgeting and financial planning.

Keeping comprehensive financial records can be beneficial when seeking funding or loans for your real estate ventures. Lenders and investors often require detailed financial information to assess the risk and potential return on their investment. Therefore, having these records readily available can expedite the process and increase your chances of securing the necessary funding.

Maintaining meticulous records of your financial transactions is a crucial aspect of successful real estate investing. It helps monitor investment performance, guides decision-making, ensures tax compliance, and can assist in securing future funding. Here's a list of possible records to maintain and keep up to date:

- Property acquisition documents
  - Purchase agreement and closing statements
  - Mortgage documents
  - Deed of ownership

- Rental income records
  - Rent receipts or records of rental payments received
  - Security deposit records

- Financial statements
  - Monthly, quarterly, and annual financial statements
  - Bank statements for property-related accounts
  - Profit and loss statements
  - Utility bills
- Property management records
  - Rental applications and background check results
  - Correspondence with tenants
  - Lease agreements including documentation of rent increase notices and tenant acknowledgments
  - Records of capital improvements, receipts for renovations and upgrades
  - Property insurance policies and insurance premium payments
  - Records of property inspections and maintenance and repair logs
  - Permits and licenses for construction work
  - Records of safety inspections and compliance with local regulations
- Tax records
  - Property taxes paid
  - Copies of filed tax returns
  - Property-related deductions and expenses
  - 1099 forms for rental income
  - Records of property depreciation for tax purposes

Keeping these records organized and up-to-date will help you effectively manage your real estate investments, ensure compliance with tax laws, and make informed financial decisions. It's advisable to consult with a financial or legal professional for guidance on record-keeping practices specific to your real estate portfolio and local regulations.

Review and Adapt

The process of reviewing your progress and adapting your business based on your findings is a crucial part of any successful venture, including real estate investment. It involves evaluating your actions, achievements, and progress toward your goals at regular intervals such as the end of each day or week. This practice enables you to stay aligned with your objectives, identify areas for improvement, and make necessary adjustments to your strategies and tasks.

Reviewing your accomplishments regularly helps you understand whether you're making progress toward your goals. By assessing what you've achieved, you can measure your performance and determine if you're on the right track. This could involve reviewing completed tasks, deals closed, or income generated in relation to your set targets. This practice also gives you an opportunity to celebrate your successes, no matter how small. Recognizing and appreciating your achievements can boost your motivation and confidence, fostering a positive mindset that can propel you toward bigger goals.

And, this review process can also highlight areas where you may be falling short. Perhaps certain tasks are taking longer than expected, or specific strategies aren't producing the desired results. Rather than viewing these as failures, use them as learning opportunities to understand what isn't working and why.

This leads to the second part of the process—adaptation. Once you've identified areas for improvement, don't be afraid to adjust your strategies and tasks as needed. This could mean adopting new approaches, learning new skills, or seeking advice from more experienced investors. Remember, the path to success is rarely a straight line, and being flexible and adaptable in your approach can help you navigate challenges and seize new opportunities.

Review and adaptation should be an ongoing process. The real estate market is dynamic and constantly changing, so it's important to continually reassess your strategies and adapt to new trends and market conditions. This proactive approach can help you stay ahead of the competition and maximize your investment returns.

Chapter 10

Finding Lucrative On- and Off-Market Deals

We firmly believe that diversifying your investment strategy can turbo-boost your real estate portfolio. Whether you're looking at openly listed properties or hidden off-market deals, you have countless opportunities, just like the numerous stars in the sky. Our aim in this chapter is to provide you with the knowledge and strategies you need to discover these opportunities and make the most of your investments.

First we discuss on-market properties. These are the properties displayed for everyone to see, much like the shiny new cars for sale on a lot. They offer a clear-cut buying process, making them a crowd favorite. However, being in the limelight means they often spark intense competition, akin to an auction for that ideal dream home.

Next, we venture into the elusive territory of off-market deals. These are the secret gold mines hidden from plain sight, waiting for the astute investor to uncover. Off-market properties often turn out to be hidden treasures that can be nabbed at potentially lower prices because they escape mainstream attention and thus attract less competition. What makes them off-market? Well, it could be due to a seller looking to make a quick sale, encountering financial hurdles, or simply desiring a more private transaction. These unique situations can pave the way for golden investment opportunities for buyers like you.

The true charm of navigating both on- and off-market paths is the opportunity to optimize your chances of finding lucrative deals while spreading your risk. Overinvesting in one area can be dicey. By diversifying, you're avoiding the pitfall of putting all your eggs in one basket. Instead, you're tactically positioning yourself to reap the benefits of both worlds—the easy access of on-market properties and the undiscovered windfalls of the off-market.

Whether you're a veteran investor or just dipping your toes into the investment waters, we're here to guide you through this ever-changing terrain. We'll explore strategies for spotting and securing these profitable real estate investments, both in the spotlight and behind the scenes.

On-Market Opportunities

On-market opportunities refers to properties that are publicly listed for sale, usually through real estate brokerage platforms, the Multiple Listing Service (MLS), or realtor agencies. These properties are visible to a wide audience of potential buyers, fostering a competitive market environment. The advantage of on-market properties is the transparency of the transaction process. All necessary details about the property, including price, location, condition, and history, are usually available for scrutiny. This open information aids in making informed decisions, albeit in a competitive setting.

The open market offers a plethora of opportunities for investors to find their next real estate venture. With a variety of online portals, such as Zillow, Trulia, and Realtor.com, potential buyers who do not have a real estate license to access the MLS can access detailed property listings with ease. These platforms provide filters that enable you to narrow down your search based on factors like location, price range, and property type. Furthermore, working with a real estate agent can provide valuable insights and access to exclusive listings that are not available publicly. By partnering with experienced professionals who have their finger on the pulse of the market, investors can uncover opportunities that align with their investment goals.

Advantages of On-Market Opportunities

On-market opportunities come with one major advantage: they are easy to find. They offer a higher degree of transparency. All necessary information is typically readily accessible, enabling investors to make informed decisions. The transaction process is usually well established and streamlined, providing a sense of security and predictability for both buyers and sellers.

Disadvantages of On-Market Opportunities

The primary drawback is the high level of competition. Due to widespread visibility, there may be numerous interested buyers, both investors and non-investors, making it more difficult to secure a property. This competition can also drive prices up, potentially reducing the profitability of the investment. Additionally, the straightforward nature of on-market transactions often leaves less room for negotiation compared to off-market deals. Last, the process can be time-consuming because buyers may need to navigate through a large volume of listings and conduct thorough due diligence on each potential investment.

Should You Hire a Real Estate Agent for On-Market Properties?

Are you thinking of handling on-market properties and not sure if you should hire a real estate agent or become one yourself? Being a real estate agent comes with some pretty cool perks, especially when it comes to finding investment opportunities in the on-market space. One of the biggest is that you get direct access to the MLS. This is a tool that gathers all property listings together and gives you detailed info on each one. It's a bit like having a huge database of properties at your fingertips, letting you spot potential investments before everyone else does. Most top real estate websites pull their info from MLSs across the country, so engaging a real estate agent who can give you firsthand access to the MLS can give you a head start.

In addition, real estate agents are the social butterflies of the property world. They build networks within the community, which often means they get early tip-offs about properties about to hit the market. Plus, they're usually in the know about the latest real estate trends and what's happening in the market, which can be a big help when making strategic investment decisions.

Also, real estate agents know their stuff when it comes to assessing a property's potential. They can walk investors through a detailed analysis of a property, looking at everything from its location and condition to its price and market trends. This can really help reduce the risk that comes with investing.

Real estate agents are pros at negotiating. They know the ins and outs of the market and how to use that knowledge to negotiate better prices and terms. This can give you a major leg up in the competitive world of on-market investment.

And last, if you're thinking about getting your license to aid in your investing, having a real estate license can significantly reduce costs. As an agent, you'll earn a commission on each property you buy or sell, which means you can recoup some or all of your investment.

Fun Fact About the MLS

Eric remembers the days before internet listing portals and the MLS as we know it now. Back then, there were no fancy digital listings or online property tours to make things easy. Instead of browsing through properties on our smartphones, real estate pros had to deal with these massive books that were like encyclopedias of real estate.

To show properties to potential buyers, agents had to rely on physical copies and make calls for each property inquiry. They had to dial up property owners or listing agents, and if a place was no longer available, they'd dramatically cross it out with a big, bold x in the book. Talk about old-school!

But now, thanks to technology, things have taken a 180-degree turn. Real estate investors have a much easier gig. With just a few clicks, they can check property status, set up viewings, or even offer virtual tours. No more lugging around heavy books, endless phone calls, or crossing out listings.

Understanding Off-Market Deals

You might think that the real estate investment game is all about browsing through listings, but let us let you in on a little secret: some of the juiciest opportunities are waiting off the beaten path. We're talking about off-market properties.

So, what are these off-market wonders, you ask? Well, they're properties that aren't shouting "For Sale!" from the rooftops. You won't find them on the usual websites or in the real estate agent's window. Nope, these are the properties that fly under the radar, and they're like the VIP section of the real estate world.

How do you stumble on off-market deals? Well, it's not by browsing Zillow or Realtor.com, that's for sure. Off-market deals come about in all sorts of ways. Sometimes, it's because you've got connections in the real estate world—a friend of a friend who knows someone looking to sell. Other times, it's simply word-of-mouth—your neighbor hears that someone down the block is thinking about moving. Then there are the sellers themselves, who decide they want to skip the whole traditional listing process and go directly to potential buyers.

Because off-market deals aren't plastered all over the internet, they're kind of like insider secrets. They're exclusive, and that makes them less competitive. Imagine this: You're at an auction, and everyone's bidding on the same painting. It gets intense. Now, picture yourself at a private art show with just a handful of people, and you're the only one interested in a hidden masterpiece. That's the difference between on-market and off-market properties.

Off-market deals are often more relaxed, with less frenzy and pressure. They're like finding a rare vinyl record in a dusty old thrift store while everyone else is lining up for the latest chart-topping album. You're not battling it out with 100 other buyers. Instead, you have the space to negotiate and secure a sweet deal.

Advantages of Off-Market Opportunities

One of the significant advantages of off-market opportunities is the reduced competition. Because these properties are not publicly listed, it limits the number of potential buyers, providing you with more negotiation power and a higher likelihood of securing the deal. This aspect also contributes to more efficient transactions: without multiple buyers bidding on the same property, the process can be quicker and less complicated because you're dealing directly with the seller.

Another advantage is the potential for better deals. Sellers who opt for off-market sales might be in a hurry to sell their property, making them more open to price negotiations. This scenario could lead to a lower purchase price compared to what you'd find on the open market. Last, off-market sales often include unique properties that owners prefer not to list publicly due to privacy reasons, giving you access to opportunities you wouldn't find on traditional listings.

Disadvantages of Off-Market Opportunities

On the flip side, off-market opportunities come with some drawbacks. One of the primary disadvantages is the limited selection. Because these properties aren't publicly listed, there may be fewer options available compared to the open market. This could mean that you have to compromise on your preferences or wait longer to find the right opportunity.

The lack of transparency is another issue with off-market deals. Sellers are able to change their selling price at last minute because it has not been published on the MLS. And there's usually less information available about the property, which could lead to potential oversights and risks.

Finally, without competition to drive up the price, there's a risk of overpaying if you're not careful. It's crucial to do your due diligence to ensure you're getting a fair deal. Although off-market opportunities can present unique advantages, they also come with their own set of challenges. As with any investment strategy, thorough research and professional advice are key.

Finding Off-Market Opportunities

Finding off-market opportunities does require a bit more time and thought compared to on-market ones. But don't worry, there are several methods you can use, even though they might be a tad more involved.

Networking

One of the most effective ways of finding off-market opportunities is through networking. Real estate professionals, friends, family, and acquaintances may have information about properties that aren't listed publicly. Attending industry events and joining real estate investment clubs can help investors make connections that could lead to off-market deals.

Imagine you're at a Sunday service or a parent-teacher association (PTA) meeting, and in the middle of a conversation, someone mentions a property that's about to hit the market. Just like that, you've stumbled on a potential real estate opportunity without even trying! It's not about attending stuffy corporate events (though they do have their perks). It's about connecting with people from all walks of life who could open doors to hidden properties.

Friends and family should be the first people you talk to about your interest in real estate. They're connected to a network of people who might just have the property lead you're looking for. Whenever you're catching up with someone, let them know about your interest in real estate. You never know what opportune information might come up! And because they are so familiar with you, feel free to make direct asks: "Do you know of anyone who needs to sell their home?" "Are there any properties that you know of that need to be fixed up, and their owners may be open to selling?" It's a lot simpler to ask these kinds of questions directly to your Aunt Jeannie or Uncle Johnny.

Moving beyond friends and family, community groups and interest groups are your next best bet for finding off-market real estate opportunities. These are the places where the true potential unfolds.

Community groups can range from hobby clubs to houses of worship, neighborhood associations, and service organizations. These platforms bring people together, fostering an environment where information is exchanged freely, including details about available properties. For instance, PTA meetings are often hubs of community news and gossip, making them potentially rich sources of leads on properties that aren't officially on the market. Similarly, houses of worship often form close-knit communities where members assist each other in various ways, which could include sharing information about available properties.

Interest groups related to your hobbies can also be fruitful. If you're a gardening enthusiast, local gardening clubs might be a good place to network and hear about properties for sale before they hit the general market.

Service organizations, which are dedicated to assisting certain causes or communities, can also provide networking opportunities. Members of these organizations often share resources and information, which might include leads on off-market properties. So, don't underestimate the power of community and interest groups. They can be your key to uncovering those hidden properties.

Overall, the beauty of the real estate market lies in the power of personal connections. People are more inclined to share information about off-market deals with individuals they trust and share a bond with. This stems from the innate human desire to help others. When someone in your network knows about an off-market deal, they are more likely to let you in on it due to the personal connection they have with you. This mutual exchange not only benefits you but also gives them a sense of satisfaction for being able to assist. Remember, the essence of networking is not always about what you can get, but also about building relationships and helping each other along the way. So, always cherish and nurture these personal connections because they are the ones that can lead you to those hidden off-market real estate gems.

The final frontier in your face-to-face networking journey is connecting with other real estate professionals. These individuals—realtors, brokers, appraisers, and even other investors—are the custodians of the property world, privy to insider market information. Establishing relationships with them can open doors to off-market opportunities that aren't available to the general public.

If you haven't already connected with these industry insiders, local investment clubs and real estate industry events serve as ideal meeting grounds. Think of these as your backstage pass to the real estate spectacle, where you'll mingle with experienced investors and fellow enthusiasts. Such platforms often morph into hubs for sharing exclusive deals and invaluable experiences.

As we navigate through a post-COVID world, don't shy away from face-to-face interactions. There's always a place for online networking, but nothing cements a connection more effectively than in-person communication. So, step out there and engage with people in real life.

Case Study: The Peculiar Ladybug Guy

Eric often shares a story about the person who taught him the art of networking. That person was none other than his maternal grandfather, Gene, a shrewd businessman with a charming quirk. Whenever he ventured into important networking events, Gene would embellish his suit with a petite yet lifelike ceramic ladybug stick pin on his shoulder.

Now, you might wonder why he chose a ladybug as his signature accessory. Well, this little ladybug held a remarkable secret; it was a conversation starter. Without fail, at every gathering, someone would approach Gene, believing that the ladybug had serendipitously landed on him. They would gently attempt to brush it off, not wanting to harm the lovable bug, fully expecting it to fly away.

Much to their surprise, the ladybug would remain firmly to its spot. The intrigued guests would invariably strike up a conversation with Eric's grandfather. Laughter and camaraderie would blossom, all thanks to that unassuming ladybug.

(continued)

(continued)

But the true beauty was in what happened next. Gene had a collection of miniature ladybug pins, identical to the one on his shoulder. With a warm and generous smile, he would reach into his pocket, unveiling a tiny ladybug pin for his newfound friend. These ladybug pins were more than mere trinkets; they were symbols of connection and friendship.

Gene became known as "the ladybug guy," which made him impossible to forget. His network thrived, and he cultivated valuable contacts that opened doors to numerous opportunities.

You don't necessarily need a collection of ladybug pins, but understanding the importance of conversation and connection can be a game-changer in your networking endeavors. Just like Eric's grandfather, you, too, can make lasting impressions and forge meaningful relationships that pave the way to success.

Social Media Networking

Like we just said, there is a time and place for social media networking. The digital world is a vast, interconnected space teeming with potential leads; you just need to know where to look! Also, it helps you network outside of your local area. If you live in North Carolina but are buying properties across the border in South Carolina, using social media makes the distance between the two a lot shorter and puts you in front of people local to your investment area. There are many articles and YouTube videos on how to use them for the real estate investment industry. Start with these three popular social networking platforms:

- **Facebook.** This platform isn't just for sharing cute cat videos. It's a hub for various community groups where members often post about properties for sale in their area. Join groups, engage with posts, and don't be shy to ask if anyone knows about available properties. Remember, your next lead could be just a post away!

- **LinkedIn.** Often overlooked in the real estate world, LinkedIn can be a goldmine of networking opportunities. Connect with real estate professionals, join real estate–focused groups, or even use the job board to find companies looking for real estate investors. Keep an eye on the Events section, too, as there are often webinars and online conferences that can help expand your knowledge and network.

- **Instagram.** This picture platform is great for finding real estate agents and property developers. They often showcase their properties on their profiles, giving you a sneak peek into potential investment opportunities. Plus, regularly engaging with their content can help you build a rapport that might lead to off-market deals.

Driving for Dollars and Direct Outreach

"Driving for dollars" is an old but gold strategy for finding potential investment properties. Imagine you're on a Sunday drive through a local neighborhood and you spot a house that's seen better days. It might be rundown or even vacant. That's your cue! This property could be a diamond in the rough, waiting for an investor like you to polish it up and make it shine again. So, how do you go from admiring from afar to making an offer?

That's where direct outreach comes in. It's just like it sounds—reaching out directly to the owner of a property you're interested in. You're cutting out the middleperson and going straight to the source. But how do you find who these owners are? That's where a little detective work comes in. Property tax records and public databases can be your best friends. They're full of information, often including contact details for property owners. In essence, direct outreach involves a fair bit of research, networking, and initiative. But the potential rewards make it a worthwhile strategy in the world of real estate investment.

Case Study: Cruising for the Perfect Fixer-Upper

A great example of driving for dollars is Jeff, an agent and investor who worked for us a few years ago. A few years back, Jeff, was on a summer vacation visiting his in-laws in an upscale neighborhood. Now, you might think that high-end areas are off-limits for real estate investments, but not Jeff. He had the investment itch and couldn't resist exploring the possibilities in this well-to-do neighborhood.

As Jeff cruised through the streets lined with perfectly manicured lawns and impressive homes, he figured he'd be hard-pressed to find a deal in this upscale neighborhood. But then, something caught his eye—a massive colonial house that stuck out like a sore thumb. Its peeling paint, overgrown grass, and cluttered backyard screamed "distressed property" amidst all the luxury.

This piqued Jeff's interest, and he decided to dig deeper. He knew that often, hidden treasures are in plain sight. So, he hopped on the local municipal website to dig up tax records on the property. Armed with this info, he tracked down the owner—a senior citizen struggling to maintain the massive property due to her age. Her kids were too far away to lend a hand, which explained the house's sorry state.

Jeff saw an opportunity here. He sat down with the owner and negotiated a deal that was fair for her but still below the market rate. This not only helped the elderly lady avoid the long process of putting the house on the market but also put Jeff in the driver's seat.

Over the following months, Jeff poured his time and resources into a makeover. He fixed up the exterior, gave the interior a modern facelift, and turned the wild backyard into a charming garden. When the renovations were done, the once-neglected house was now modern and blended seamlessly into the rest of the neighborhood.

(continued)

(continued)

When Jeff put the property on the market, it didn't take long for it to find a new owner. With this sale Jeff turned a tidy profit. But it wasn't just about the money—it was also about solving a problem for the elderly owner and restoring the home to suit the neighborhood's charm.

Jeff's story is a key example of why it pays to always be on the lookout for investment opportunities, no matter where you are. It's about doing your homework, finding connections, and turning neglected properties into success stories. So, the next time you're cruising around your neighborhood or even a neighborhood you've never been in, keep your eyes peeled—you might just stumble on your very own hidden fixer-upper.

Divorce Attorneys and Estate Agents

Divorces are tough, and often result in properties being sold quickly, usually at a reduced price. Networking with divorce attorneys can put you in a prime position to learn about such opportunities. Similar to divorce attorneys, estate agents deal with properties that often need to be sold quickly due to the owner's death. This urgency can translate into bargain prices for investors.

Contractors and Builders

These professionals are often the first to know when a property is about to go on the market—even before real estate agents. By keeping in touch with contractors and builders, you could get a head start on upcoming listings. Our buddy Mike, a contractor, once tipped Eric off about a property his client wanted to sell at our annual holiday party. Being in direct contact with Mike put Eric first in line when it came to negotiating a deal.

Pre-Foreclosures

Pre-foreclosure is an interesting period in the life cycle of a property. This stage kicks off when a homeowner starts missing mortgage payments—usually about three to six months' worth. The lender, at this point, issues a notice of default, essentially a warning shot to the homeowner that their property is on the brink of foreclosure.

Now, here's where the opportunity arises. The pre-foreclosure stage provides homeowners with a window to sell their property before it gets foreclosed by the bank. This is often a distressed sale, meaning the property might be available at a price lower than the market rate. For you as an investor, it could be a golden chance to secure a property below its market value.

But how do you find these properties? Pre-foreclosure notices are a matter of public record and can be found at your local county courthouse or sometimes even online. Also, some websites like Zillow, RealtyTrac, and PreForclosure can provide listings of pre-foreclosure homes. Though some of these platforms charge a small fee, they aggregate data from various sources, making it easier for you to find potential deals.

■ ■ ■

We believe that the world of real estate investment offers a multitude of opportunities, both on and off the market. Whether you choose the well-trodden path of on-market properties or venture into the hidden world of off-market deals, the key to success lies in diversification and strategic decision-making.

On-market properties provide transparency and ease of access, making them suitable for investors seeking a straightforward buying process. However, they come with fierce competition and potential price inflation due to their high visibility. Nevertheless, with the right guidance from real estate professionals, you can navigate this landscape effectively.

However, off-market opportunities offer reduced competition, potential for better deals, and unique properties that owners prefer to keep private. Networking plays a pivotal role in discovering these hidden gems, whether through personal connections, industry professionals, or online platforms. It's the power of personal relationships that often leads to off-market opportunities, so nurture those connections.

Direct outreach strategies like driving for dollars and targeting pre-foreclosure properties can also yield fruitful results. These methods require initiative, research, and networking but can lead to properties with substantial investment potential.

In the world of real estate investing, opportunities abound, and success comes to those who are willing to diversify their strategies, build relationships, and stay vigilant for hidden opportunities. Whether you're a seasoned investor or just starting, the pursuit of lucrative on and off-market deals is rewarding and can help you achieve your real estate investment goals.

Chapter 11

The Big Winner!

Value-Add Real Estate

Value-add investing in real estate is the process of discovering untapped potential and then leveraging that potential to its fullest extent. Think of value-add investing in real estate like a treasure hunt. You're searching for a property that others might overlook, a diamond in the rough. Just like a jeweler who takes an uncut gem and carefully shapes it to reveal its true beauty, you're looking to uncover the hidden potential in a property.

Eric firmly believes in the transformative power of value-add real estate investments. He sees it as more than just a way to make money. To him, it's an art. It's about having the vision to see what a property could be, the creativity to imagine the possibilities, and the financial savvy to make it all happen. When Eric finds a fixer-upper, his eyes light up like a kid on Christmas morning. He loves nothing more than rolling up his sleeves and planning out how to turn that diamond in the rough into a sparkling gem.

That passion of his? It's infectious. Whether he's mentoring newcomers to the field or penning his latest book, he's always talking about value-add investing. According to him, there's no better, or more satisfying way to build wealth in the real estate market. In this chapter, we share an insider's guide to what we consider the most lucrative form of real estate investing: added value!

The Magic of Value-Add Investing

What makes value-add real estate investing so exciting is that it's not just about making a property look pretty. Investing in these properties is a powerful way to generate income and grow your capital. How does it work? Well, you start by finding properties that are already bringing in some cash flow. But here's the kicker—with a few well-planned improvements, these properties could be making a lot more money.

Often they're rundown—not because of any inherent flaw, but because the owners lack either the cash or the wherewithal to implement necessary improvements. Or maybe, they just don't know the real potential of what they own, leading to sheer neglect. Now, this is where you as an investor can swoop in and make a killing! You can acquire such distressed or value-add properties at a price that's often significantly below market.

So, how do you add value to a property? There are loads of ways. Maybe the building needs a bit of a facelift or an extension to add more space. Or perhaps the management practices need to be shaken up a bit. You could also consider upgrading the state of the property, giving the interiors a makeover, or working on getting more tenants in. The sky's the limit really, and that's what makes it so thrilling!

Let's say you find a worn-down apartment building in a great location. It's generating some income, but there's room for improvement. This is where the magic of value-add investing comes into play. It's not just about buying and holding. It's about enhancing the asset to boost its income generation and capital growth.

You roll up your sleeves and start making changes. Maybe you renovate the units, adding modern fixtures and fresh paint. Or you could add amenities like a gym or a rooftop deck that attracts more tenants. Perhaps you improve the management practices, ensuring quicker response times to tenant requests.

The ultimate objective is straightforward yet potentially lucrative: amplify the property's income-generating potential and subsequently sell or refinance it at a price higher than your original investment.

Though it necessitates effort, strategic foresight, and occasionally a dash of creativity, the potential returns can render this approach exceedingly worthwhile. Therefore, if you're prepared to embrace the challenge and actively participate, value-add investing in commercial real estate could be a profitable expedition.

Investing in Multifamily and Commercial Real Estate

Value-add investing truly shines in several areas, but two exciting sectors offer a vast landscape of untapped potential: multifamily and commercial real estate. Multifamily investments are your gateway into the residential real estate market. Consider a rundown multifamily building or an apartment building. With some strategic upgrades, efficient management, and a dash of creativity, you can transform it into a sought-after residence, drastically driving up rental income and property value.

However, commercial real estate can offer a wide range of opportunity. Think of outdated office buildings, underused retail spaces, or even abandoned warehouses. With the right vision and strategic investment, these can be transformed into thriving business centers, bustling shopping precincts, or even trendy loft-style apartments.

Benefits of Multifamily Properties

Starting small is often the key to monumental success. Dipping your toes into the vast ocean of real estate investing? Consider starting with buildings of four family units or less. These smaller multifamily properties are the perfect entry point for budding investors, providing a manageable and tangible introduction to the business of property management and value-add strategies. As we've mentioned, buildings with four or fewer family units are often classified as residential properties. This presents a fantastic opportunity for you to dip your toes into the world of real estate investment with properties that fall into a category familiar to most people.

More Doors, More Money

In the realm of real estate, doors are more than just an architectural feature. When we say *doors*, we're referring to the number of units a person owns. Each door represents a separate income-generating unit within a property, and every door adds to the total potential income of your real estate portfolio. If an investor says they own 20 doors, this could mean they own a 20-unit apartment building or perhaps five 4-unit multifamily buildings. More doors, more opportunities for rental income and wealth generation.

Qualify for Residential Loans

Properties classified as residential open up a unique opportunity for investors because they usually qualify for residential loans. Now, why is this beneficial? The answer lies in the terms of residential loans compared to their commercial counterparts. Residential loans are designed for individuals buying homes to live in rather than businesses investing in commercial properties. Because of this, lenders often offer more favorable terms on these loans.

For starters, residential loans tend to have lower interest rates. This means the cost of borrowing is less, reducing your monthly repayments and the overall amount you'll pay back over the life of the loan. This can significantly increase the profitability of your investment.

In addition to lower interest rates, residential loans also often come with more flexible terms. For example, they may offer longer repayment periods, which can further reduce your monthly payments. Some residential loans even offer options for early repayment without penalties, giving you the flexibility to pay off your loan sooner if you're able to.

Furthermore, the qualification process for residential loans can be easier than for commercial loans. Lenders look at personal credit scores and income, which can be less daunting for new investors compared to the complex financial evaluations required for commercial loans.

So, by investing in properties classified as residential, you could potentially take advantage of these more favorable loan conditions. This makes such properties an excellent choice for those new to real estate investing or those looking for a more cost-effective financing option.

Easier to Manage

When it comes to the management of multifamily properties, smaller buildings, such as those with four or fewer units, offer a distinct advantage. Simply put, they are easier to manage. The most obvious advantage is that there are fewer tenants to deal with. This means fewer personalities, fewer requests, and fewer potential conflicts to navigate. It also means less time spent on administrative tasks like collecting rent, addressing tenant concerns, and filling vacancies.

Second, maintenance and upkeep become more manageable with a smaller property. With fewer units, there's less square footage to maintain and fewer appliances that could potentially break down. You can more easily keep track of what needs to be done and when it needs to be done. This enables you to maintain a high standard of quality for the property, which is essential in attracting and retaining tenants.

Last, smaller multifamily properties provide a great learning ground for new investors. They enable you to gain hands-on experience with property management without being overwhelmed by the scale of it. You'll learn how to deal with tenants, how to handle repairs and maintenance, and how to navigate the financial aspects of property ownership. These skills will be invaluable if you decide to invest in larger properties in the future.

Demand Is Soaring

Small multifamily properties such as duplexes, triplexes, and four-plexes are experiencing a surge in demand, especially in urban and suburban areas with high population density. There are several reasons behind this trend. One key reason is affordability. Housing that is affordable for low- and moderate-income households is in short supply in both rural and urban communities. Smaller multifamily homes present a more affordable option for many households compared to single-family homes, particularly in densely populated areas where land and housing costs are high.

Furthermore, zoning changes in many cities are allowing for higher residential density, which means more multifamily developments such as duplexes, triplexes, and fourplexes are permitted. This is creating more opportunities for investors to meet the growing demand.

Another factor driving demand is the shift in preference toward vibrant, diverse, sustainable, and walkable urban living spaces. Duplexes, triplexes, and fourplexes often fit this bill, offering residents the benefits of both apartment living and home ownership. This high demand ensures a steady stream of rental income for investors. With more people seeking out these types of properties, vacancy rates tend to be lower. And even when a unit does become vacant, there's usually a pool of potential tenants ready to move in. This makes small multifamily properties a dependable asset class for real estate investment.

Moreover, the demand for such properties doesn't show signs of slowing down soon. With ongoing urbanization and changes in housing preferences, duplexes, triplexes, and fourplexes are likely to remain a hot commodity in the real estate market. This provides investors with not only steady rental income but also the potential for capital appreciation over time.

Potential for Appreciation

Appreciation, or the increase in a property's value over time, is a key component of real estate investing. For small multifamily properties like duplexes, triplexes, and fourplexes, there's substantial potential for appreciation.

One way to boost the value of these properties is through strategic upgrades. This could include cosmetic improvements like painting, flooring, and landscaping, or more significant renovations such as updating kitchens and bathrooms, improving energy efficiency, or adding amenities like laundry facilities or outdoor spaces. Upgrades not only make a property more attractive to potential tenants but also they can allow you to charge higher rent, boosting your income in the short term. Over the long term, these improvements can significantly enhance the property's resale value.

Efficient management is another key to enhancing a property's value. Good property management involves keeping the property well maintained, minimizing vacancies, and building positive relationships with tenants. A well-managed property is more likely to retain its value and attract quality tenants who are willing to pay higher rents.

Another factor that can contribute to appreciation is the location of the property. Properties in desirable neighborhoods or in areas experiencing economic growth and development are likely to see their values rise over time. When the time is right to sell, you could achieve a higher resale value, resulting in a significant return on your investment.

Case Study: Maximizing Returns—Strategic Renovations

Nina is a real estate investor in a gentrifying city in New Jersey. Last year she came across a promising four-family property being offered under market value. The property, owned by an elderly man who had put in only the bare minimum maintenance over the years, included a small unpaved lot.

Seeing the potential in the property, Nina purchased it with a vision to transform it into a desirable residential space. After purchasing, she modernized each of the four apartments. Old appliances were replaced with new, energy-efficient ones. The walls received a fresh coat of paint, and outdated fixtures were swapped out for modern ones. Nina also added washer-dryer hookups to each apartment, a convenience that prospective tenants would certainly appreciate.

(continued)

(continued)

However, the most significant upgrade was outside the building. Recognizing the premium on parking spaces in the crowded neighborhood, Nina decided to pave the small attached lot and convert it into a parking area. This strategic improvement not only increased the property's value but also offered a unique selling point for potential tenants.

Once the renovations were complete, Nina didn't just rent out the apartments; she also rented out the parking spots. Each tenant was given the option to rent a spot for an additional fee. But Nina's ingenuity didn't stop there. With a few parking spots left over, she approached the neighboring convenience store and offered to rent them the remaining spaces for their customers. The store owner, aware of the constant struggle for parking in the area, readily agreed.

Beyond the physical improvements, Nina revolutionized the management of the building. She implemented an online management system, streamlining the process for her tenants. The previous owner had done everything manually. Cash or check payments, phone calls for service requests—it was impossible for both the owner and the tenants to keep track of all their needs and communications. This new tech platform enabled tenants to pay rent online, submit service requests, and track all their transactions and interactions within their own accounts. This efficient system not only made life easier for her tenants but also simplified the administrative side of property management for Nina.

After all the strategic renovations and efficient management, the value of Nina's four-family property soared. The property's worth increased by over $300,000, a testament to Nina's foresight and hard work. Seeing the growth in her investment, she decided to refinance the property. By doing so, she was able to cash out a significant amount while still retaining ownership of the property.

Now, with a substantial sum at her disposal and the successful transformation of the four-family property under her belt, Nina set her sights on new investment opportunities. She was ready to

(continued)

replicate her success, scouting for the next diamond in the rough that she could transform into a profitable real estate investment.

Nina's story serves as an inspiration to aspiring real estate investors. It demonstrates the power of strategic renovations, efficient management, and smart financial decisions. With the right approach and a keen eye for potential, it's indeed possible to significantly enhance the value of a property and reap substantial rewards.

Benefits of Commercial Properties

Value-added commercial real estate investing is a strategic approach that focuses on acquiring properties with potential for enhancement on a much larger scale than residential. The essence of this strategy is to generate returns by proactively improving the value of a commercial real estate asset and increasing its income potential.

Anything over a four-family building is typically deemed commercial. You might be wondering why that distinction matters. Well, this classification opens up an exciting world of opportunities for value-added investing. Imagine owning a 20-unit apartment building and being able to elevate its potential with your creativity, strategic management, and financial acumen. With such a significant number of units, even small improvements can lead to substantial increases in cash flow. It's like hitting the jackpot in the wealth-creation lottery!

As discussed, a value-add property often has some minor blemishes, be it physical issues that need repairing or management inefficiencies that can be streamlined. These properties typically have in place cash flow, but the goal is to increase that cash flow over time through strategic improvement. Let's consider an example. Suppose you purchase an office building that's only 70% occupied due to outdated interiors and lack of modern amenities. As a value-add investor, you could renovate the building, install modern fixtures, and maybe even add shared amenities like a conference room or lounge. Once these improvements are made, the property could attract more tenants, enabling you to increase rental rates and occupancy levels, thus boosting the property's overall income and value.

Another example is a retail strip center with high vacancy rates due to poor management or lack of visibility. By investing in better signage, enhancing curb appeal, and implementing an effective marketing strategy, you could attract high-quality tenants and reduce vacancies.

The value can be added to all types of commercial real estate, including office buildings, multifamily units, logistics properties, and retail spaces. The key is to identify properties where strategic improvements can lead to increased cash flow and property value.

High Demand, High Returns: Warehouse Investments

Warehouses are currently in high demand! The rise of e-commerce and changes in consumer behavior have catapulted the need for extensive and efficient warehouse spaces. A warehouse isn't just a storage unit anymore; it's the beating heart of the supply chain system.

Strategic improvements in a warehouse can significantly enhance its functionality and appeal to potential tenants, resulting in increased rental income and property value. For instance, upgrading the loading docks to accommodate more or larger trucks can improve logistics efficiency. Installing advanced inventory management systems and automation technologies can optimize storage use, making the warehouse more attractive to businesses seeking high-tech facilities. Moreover, improvements such as energy-efficient lighting and HVAC systems not only reduce operating costs but also make the property more sustainable and appealing in today's green-conscious market.

These value-added strategies can transform a traditional warehouse into a modern, efficient, and sustainable facility, creating a win-win situation for both the investor and the tenant. The warehouse sector, once overlooked, has now emerged as a promising arena for value-added real estate investing.

Higher Income Potential

Overall, commercial properties often provide higher income potential compared to residential ones. The rent for commercial properties is typically calculated per square foot, which can lead to higher returns, especially in prime locations. Plus, commercial leases are usually longer than residential ones, providing a more stable and predictable income stream.

When it comes to commercial real estate, the value is largely driven by the amount of income it generates. This income usually comes in the form of rent paid by tenants occupying the property. Appraisers and investors typically use a method called the *capitalization rate* (or cap rate, discussed in Chapter 5) to determine the value of commercial properties. The cap rate is calculated by dividing the annual net operating income (NOI, discussed in Chapter 5) of the property by the market value of the property.

By contrast, residential real estate values are often determined by comparing the property to similar homes that have recently sold in the same area. This is known as the comparative market analysis (CMA, also discussed in Chapter 5) approach.

Now, this difference in valuation methods gives commercial real estate investors a unique advantage. Suppose you own a commercial property and decide to make strategic improvements, such as renovating the interiors or adding amenities that attract higher-paying tenants. These improvements could enable you to command higher rents, increasing your NOI. And because the value of your property is directly tied to its NOI (through the cap rate), an increase in NOI can lead to a significant boost in your property's value. This is what is meant by having more control over the value of your investment in commercial real estate. You can actively take steps to increase your property's income and, thereby, its value, something that's harder to do with residential real estate, where values are more influenced by comparable sales and market conditions.

Economies of Scale

Another significant advantage of commercial real estate investments is the impressive scale they offer. *Economies of scale* is a term that refers to the cost advantage that businesses obtain due to their scale of operation or size. In the context of commercial real estate, owning a multiunit property enables you to enjoy these economies of scale in several ways.

Let's take improvements, for instance. If you own a multiunit commercial building and decide to upgrade the heating system or replace the roof, the cost of that improvement is essentially spread across all the units in the building. However, if you owned multiple single-family homes, you'd have to make those same improvements on each individual property, which could be significantly more costly on a per-unit basis.

The same principle applies to maintenance and management costs. With a multiunit commercial property, you can often have one maintenance team service the entire building and one property manager handle all tenant-related issues. This centralization can lead to significant cost savings compared to managing multiple separate residential properties, where each might require its own set of maintenance and management resources.

So, in essence, owning multiunit commercial properties can be more cost-effective because you can distribute the costs of improvements, maintenance, and management across multiple units. This can lower your per-unit costs and potentially increase your profit margins. However, it's important to note that this depends on keeping the units occupied. Vacancies can quickly erode these economies of scale.

Case Study: Skyrocketing Your Rent Roll

Eric's most cherished undertaking was a unique mixed-use property he stumbled on, which housed six apartments and four commercial spaces. The previous owners were in the midst of a divorce, desperate to offload the property quickly without the usual fanfare of inspections or restrictions. Sensing an opportunity, Eric stepped up to fill that role as the buyer.

(continued)

(continued)

The property had suffered from severe neglect due to the personal issues its owners were facing. The fallout from the divorce had led to cash flow problems, resulting in a lack of maintenance on the property. Major inspection issues arose, and high vacancy rates became a significant concern. These hurdles would have deterred a typical buyer, mainly because they would struggle to secure the necessary funding to close such a deal. But for Eric, this was a challenge he was more than willing to take on, recognizing the potential opportunities that lay ahead.

Eric saw past the property's current state, envisioning what it could become. He believed that with some hard work and strategic planning, he could double the property's value in just six months. Once he took ownership, he wasted no time in renovating all the vacant spaces, giving them a fresh, appealing look. Within two months, all spaces were rented out.

But Eric didn't stop there. He gave the entire property a thorough cleaning, followed by additional cosmetic updates. These improvements had a dramatic effect—the monthly rent roll skyrocketed from $10,000 to $20,000 in just half a year.

With the property now worth twice as much as when he first bought it, Eric was in a strong position. He approached a bank with the increased rent roll and was able to extract 70% of the property's new value. Remarkably, within six months, Eric recouped all of his initial investment. As Eric always says, "When you invest in value-added properties, you work smarter, increase your value, and count your profits!"

Considerations Before Jumping into Commercial Investing

Commercial value-added properties, like any investment, have their own set of hurdles and risks. These types of properties can be heavy on the pocket. They often need a big chunk of change upfront for renovations and improvements. Whether it's structural changes, cosmetic upgrades, or even changing the property's purpose, these costs can pile up and might exceed your budget if you're not careful.

And don't forget about the time factor. From spotting opportunities, buying properties, planning and carrying out renovations to finding tenants for the space—it's a process that can eat up a lot of your time. It needs hands-on management and an active role, which might not be everyone's cup of tea, especially if you're more of a passive investor.

Then, there's the risk that the property might not meet your expectations. Despite all the improvements, there's no guarantee that you'll be able to bump up rents or fill up the space as much as you'd hoped, and you might not get back what you invested. Commercial properties can be sensitive to how the economy is doing. If we hit a rough patch economically, businesses may struggle or go under, leading to vacant spaces or lower rents.

A perfect example of the economy effecting commercial properties was the COVID-19 pandemic. Office vacancies skyrocketed at an unprecedented level. Once thriving office buildings became ghost towns overnight as companies transitioned to remote work. Even as the world is slowly recovering, the numbers haven't returned to the pre-pandemic levels. Many investors were hit hard, with some losing a significant chunk of their investment, and others losing their properties entirely. The pandemic served as a rude awakening, demonstrating that even the most promising investments can fall victim to unforeseen circumstances.

Commercial real estate tends to be less liquid than residential properties. *Liquidity* refers to how easily an asset can be converted into cash. In the context of real estate, a market is considered liquid when properties can be sold quickly at their market value. There are a few reasons why commercial properties are less liquid than residential. For one, the pool of potential buyers is usually smaller. Commercial properties are typically more expensive and require a certain level of expertise to manage. This narrows down the number of individuals or entities who have the resources and knowledge to invest.

Another factor is the time it takes to complete a transaction. Commercial real estate transactions involve a lot of due diligence, including inspections, appraisals, and securing financing, which can extend the time it takes to close a deal. So, if you're in a situation where you need to sell your commercial property quickly, you might find it challenging to do so without accepting a lower price. This is an important risk to consider when investing in commercial real estate.

Tenant turnover is another crucial factor to think about when dealing with commercial real estate. Yes, it's true that commercial leases are typically longer-term agreements, which can provide a sense of stability and consistent cash flow for property owners. But, there's a flip side to that coin.

Imagine this: You've got a great tenant running a bustling restaurant in your property. They've signed a long-term lease, business is booming, and rent payments are coming in like clockwork. It feels like smooth sailing, right? However, what happens when that lease ends and they decide to relocate their business?

Finding a new tenant isn't always as straightforward as it might seem. Commercial tenants often have very particular requirements for their businesses. They may need specific zoning permissions, unique floor layouts, or certain structural elements. It's not like renting out a residential property where, generally speaking, if someone is looking for a two-bedroom apartment, your two-bedroom apartment will meet their needs.

With commercial properties, you could find yourself waiting for months, maybe even years, to find the right tenant whose business needs align with what your property offers. And during that time, the property isn't generating any income. So, although the longer leases in commercial real estate can be a major plus, the challenges of tenant turnover definitely add a layer of complexity.

Commercial real estate is quite the intricate puzzle compared to its residential counterpart. It's like navigating a maze with twists and turns at every corner. Take zoning laws, for instance. When dealing with residential properties, it's relatively simple—they're zoned for single-family homes or multifamily units. But in the commercial realm, things get a bit more complicated. Is the property zoned for retail, office, or industrial use? Can it accommodate mixed-use? And these zoning laws have implications for everything from parking requirements to signage restrictions. It's like trying to solve a Rubik's cube where every move matters.

And then there are environmental regulations to grapple with. This isn't just about being environmentally conscious, though that's undoubtedly important. It's also about ensuring compliance with legal requirements regarding waste disposal, air and water quality, and even potential contamination issues, particularly with industrial properties.

Finally, the terms of commercial leases add another layer of complexity. Unlike residential leases, which mainly deal with aspects like utilities and property maintenance, commercial leases delve into more intricate details. Issues such as rent escalations, build-out allowances, and lease renewal options come into play. It's like learning a new language entirely!

So, although commercial real estate may seem like a golden opportunity on the surface, it's definitely not for the fainthearted. It requires careful navigation through a labyrinth of laws, regulations, and lease terms. But, as they say, "the greater the challenge, the greater the triumph." So for those willing to take on the complexities, the rewards can be well worth the effort!

Case Study: Noelle's Secret to Choosing an Area

Noelle, having spent a large part of her career working to improve downtown areas, is a huge proponent of buying commercial properties in areas that have BIDs—business improvement districts.

A BID is a special zone where building owners chip in a bit extra in taxes or fees. And why would they do that, you ask? Well, it's all for the sake of making their district a better place to do business. You see, these extra funds are put toward things like cleaning up the streets, boosting security, sprucing up public spaces, and even marketing the area. It's like giving the district a mini makeover that goes above and beyond what the city typically provides.

(continued)

(continued)

Now, how is all this funded? The magic comes from a special assessment paid by property owners within the district. This isn't just some arbitrary number, though. It's often based on factors like property values or front footage, among other things, depending on local laws. These funds then get funneled right back into improving and enhancing the district.

Okay, so all this sounds great, but why should anyone care about BIDs? Well, if you're considering commercial investment, BIDs could make an area significantly more attractive, and here's why. First, who doesn't love improved services and infrastructure? The extra security, street cleaning, and maintenance provided by BIDs can really boost the area's appeal and functionality. It makes the area shine brighter for residents, businesses, and customers alike.

Then there's the marketing and promotion aspect. Many BIDs take it on themselves to shout from the rooftops about their district and its businesses. More foot traffic and visibility could mean a serious boost in sales and popularity in the area.

And let's not forget about community engagement. Many BIDs work tirelessly to create a real sense of community, organizing events and activities that draw crowds. This community vibe can be a big draw for businesses and customers.

But most important, there's the potential for increased property values. The various improvements and services provided by BIDs can make properties within the district more valuable. And for investors, that translates to higher potential returns.

So, you see, Noelle's passion for BIDs isn't just out of nowhere. It's rooted in her understanding of how these districts can transform a downtown area, making it more appealing not just for business owners but for everyone who spends time there. And from an investment standpoint, the potential for increased property values within BIDs is a huge plus. She's seen firsthand how the extra funding for enhanced services, marketing efforts, and

(continued)

community engagement can really pay off. So, if you're thinking about commercial investment or just want to understand what's driving the revitalization of a certain downtown area—ask city hall if there is a BID that you can contact.

Value-add investing in real estate is all about uncovering hidden gems within properties and making the most out of them. Eric is a big believer in this strategy, seeing it as an art that demands vision, creativity, and financial know-how. He gets positively charged up when he comes across a fixer-upper, thrilled at the chance to turn it into something remarkable. Eric's enthusiasm for value-add investing is infectious, whether he's guiding newcomers or sharing insights in his writing. Exploring multi-use and commercial properties can be particularly rewarding when seeking out these value-add opportunities.

Chapter 12

Common Mistakes to Avoid

Everyone will make mistakes, and making mistakes is important on your real estate investing journey. Yes, you heard us right! Mistakes are not the end of the world—not by a long shot.

We'll let you in on a little secret that many successful investors will admit freely: they've all made their fair share of blunders along the way. Some of them have even been made by us! It's like learning to ride a bike: you might wobble and even fall a few times, but that doesn't mean you won't eventually become a pro at it. See, here's the thing about mistakes in real estate investing: they're actually fantastic learning opportunities. They're like signposts on the road to success, showing you what *not* to do next time. It's all part of the process. So, don't beat yourself up over them. Learn from them.

Now, we're not saying you should go out there and make reckless decisions, thinking "Oh, it's just a mistake; no big deal!" That's not what we mean at all. Depending on the nature of the misstep, mistakes can cost time, money, and in some cases your reputation. What we are saying is, that when you do make a mistake, it's crucial to assess what went wrong, identify what other decisions you could have made that would have led to a better outcome, and, most important, don't make the same mistake again.

One of the most incredible benefits of having us as your mentor is that we're here to guide you away from the pitfalls we've encountered. It's like having a GPS that knows all the detours and traffic jams on the road to success. Picture this: You're navigating a maze, and we've been through it before. We know which paths lead to dead ends and which ones open up to treasure troves of opportunities. So, lean in, because we spill the beans on how you can avoid those pesky mistakes.

In this chapter, we offer tips and examples of mistakes that most people make when they are new to real estate investing. By noting these mistakes you will learn how to spot red flags. See, in real estate, there are signs that can alert you to potential trouble. It's like having a sixth sense for sniffing out deals that might not be as sweet as they seem. We teach you how to trust your instincts and not just see with your eyes, but also with your gut. And later in this chapter, we introduce you to Matt and Liz who jumped into real estate investing without recognizing multiple mistakes that cost them money.

Failing to Have the Right Insurance

Before you make an investment, break ground, or demo a kitchen, take the time to find an insurance agent who will clearly explain the kind of insurance coverage you need for your project. Reject the urge to indulge in wishful thoughts like, no one will get hurt, nothing will catch fire, or that water damage is unlikely. Finding an insurance company that is willing to understand the nature of your project so you have the right coverage is one of the most important steps you must take to increase your chances for success.

Additionally, during your search for potential insurers, ask how they might respond to various scenarios like fires, floods, and other acts of God. All insurance companies are not created equal. Some pay quickly, and others have an easier claim process. You must make sure that you're connecting with a firm that is going to be there for you when you need it. Your insurance carrier must be somebody who you are comfortable with.

This mistake reminded us of Mark. He was new to real estate flipping, and even though he understood that you couldn't renovate a property without insurance, he didn't do enough research on what types of insurance he needed for his project. He thought his homeowner's policy would cover everything, but he didn't realize that when you're doing extensive renovations, which he was, you need something extra, called *builder's risk insurance*.

While the renovation was in full swing, a major storm hit the area. Unfortunately, the old roof of Mark's fixer-upper couldn't handle the deluge of water. The result? Water damage. The floors were ruined, the walls were soaked, and Mark's dreams of turning a profit were quickly slipping away like water through his fingers.

It was then that Mark realized his mistake. He didn't have the right insurance to cover this kind of scenario. He was stuck with a half-renovated property, a stack of bills, and a sinking feeling of regret.

Mark learned a valuable lesson about the importance of having the right insurance in real estate. We can assure you that every property Mark has renovated since has been properly insured.

Taking on Too Much at One Time

> *My candle burns at both ends;*
> *It will not last the night;*
> *But ah, my foes, and oh, my friends—*
> *It gives a lovely light!*
>
> —*Edna St. Vincent Millay*[1]

As a child, Noelle's mom had this poem hanging over her bed. Young Noelle used to read it all the time, but its true meaning didn't hit her until she ventured into real estate investing. When you dive into the investing world, opportunities seem to pop up left and right, all at once. It can get pretty overwhelming. But one day, Noelle's mom reminded her of that poem.

Noelle had an aha moment. She realized that a full and vibrant life can be a bit complicated and sometimes overwhelming, but it's also incredibly beautiful. The key is not to burn out too quickly. Noelle hasn't stop looking at every opportunity that comes her way but she has become much more selective, picking only the ones that fit into her current life and goals.

---

[1] Edna St. Vincent Millay, *A Few Figs from Thistles: Poems and Sonnets* (New York: F. Shay, 1922). https://www.loc.gov/item/23000636.

You've done your homework, sharpened your networking skills, and joined all the right associations in your community. Now you find yourself with multiple opportunities. Resist the temptation to say yes to all of them. Sometimes you need to just focus on one opportunity at a time. Remember, there's always going to be another opportunity down the pike.

Taking on too much at one time would be our biggest mistake.

Before we truly understood the impact of this mistake, we estimate that it probably cost us 30% more for each project, and took three times as long to get any one of them done, because they were all happening at the same time. We would hire help quickly to make up for the abundance of work, but time and time again it either wasn't the right type of assistance or too late to make a difference.

Start out slowly. Get to know what type of people power you will need for various jobs. Understand the time frame of various size projects, so you can better manage your time and that of others.

Not Dotting All Your *I*s and Crossing All Your *T*s

At times, the thrill of embarking on what appears to be a promising deal can lead us to overlook or become complacent about crucial details. It's easy to get caught up in the excitement of a potential opportunity, but it's imperative to maintain a vigilant eye on essential factors. Here are a few critical details that should never be underestimated or ignored:

- **Payment with a signed contract.** Always ensure you receive the agreed-on payment, whether it's a security deposit, rent, or any other financial commitment, when the contract is signed.
- **Property inspection.** Always conduct a thorough property inspection to identify any issues or needed repairs before finalizing a deal. This prevents unexpected costs down the road.
- **Legal documents.** Thoroughly review all legal documents, including leases, contracts, and property titles. Carefully

scrutinize for any potential misunderstandings or discrepancies. It's strongly advised to seek legal counsel to ensure the accuracy and completeness of your contracts.

- **Zoning laws.** Familiarize yourself with zoning regulations and land-use laws in the area. These can significantly affect what you can and cannot do with a property.

- **Insurance requirements.** Ensure you have the necessary insurance coverage for your property, including liability and property insurance.

These details, when carefully attended to, can help you avoid costly mistakes and ensure a smoother and more profitable real estate investment experience.

Case Study: Contract Crisis—The Lease That Backfired

Not too long ago, Cole, a real estate investor, had a commercial space in a mixed-use building that he desperately wanted to rent out. After several months of tenant hunting, he was eager to get the space occupied and start generating rental income.

Finally, he found what seemed like the perfect tenant. Cole wasted no time and scheduled a meeting in his office to sign the leasing agreement. However, things took an unexpected turn when the tenant arrived without the required check for the agreed-on rent and security deposit. In a moment of trust, Cole decided to proceed with the agreement, hoping the tenant would bring the payment the next day. Both parties signed the agreement, sealing the deal.

To Cole's dismay, the next day came and went with no payment. The tenant moved into the space, even bringing in contractors for renovations, all while offering excuses for not providing the necessary funds.

(continued)

Two agonizing months passed, and the tenant had yet to deliver the security deposit, initial rent, or the additional months' rent. Frustrated and realizing he had no other option, Cole initiated eviction proceedings.

The real kicker was that Cole, by signing the agreement without securing the initial payment, had essentially trapped himself in a contract without any compensation. It was a challenging situation, but eventually, he managed to remove the tenant.

The valuable lesson Cole learned from this ordeal was crystal clear: never, under any circumstances, sign an agreement without receiving the upfront payment. It was a lesson that came at a price, but it left an indelible mark on his real estate investing journey.

Not Making Sure You Can Cover Your First Investment If Your Tenants Don't Pay Rent

It's crucial to have a financial cushion in place to cover expenses even if your tenants face difficulties in paying rent. This way, you won't find yourself in a tight spot if there's a temporary dip in rental income. Remember during the pandemic residential renters received relief from paying rent; however, landlords did not receive relief from paying their mortgages.

Not Exercising Your Due Diligence

Don't take anyone's word for anything. Always verify information independently. Don't rely solely on what others tell you. Conduct thorough research, verify documents, and seek professional advice to ensure you have accurate and reliable information.

Not Doing Your Zoning Research

Know what you're buying. Don't buy based on what is there; buy based on what the town says can be there. Understanding zoning regulations is crucial. It ensures you're aware of any restrictions or potential changes in land use that could affect your property's value or how you can use it in the future.

Eric once sold a single-family house that, at the time of closing, was zoned for multifamily buildings. Soon after the closing, the town was rezoned and the area no longer allowed for multifamily development. The investors who bought the property were counting on turning the single-family house into a two-family house. Had they done their due diligence and spoken to the town zoning department they would have discovered that the area was in the process of being rezoned. Knowing that their greatest profit would come from renovating the house into a two-family, they should have paid heed to the expression "trust, but verify."

Starting with Single-Tenant Commercial Properties

Single-tenant properties can be riskier for new investors because they are heavily dependent on the success and stability of a single business. Diversifying with multi-tenant properties can be a safer starting point.

Let's say you are able to land a large single-tenant commercial building with a major retailer. What happens if that retailer decides to close its doors? You don't have any other tenants to contribute to the mortgage, and you are the only source of payment. You are left with only a few options: invest more money into renovating the building to accommodate smaller retailers or find another large retailer who will take the whole space. The latter option can take months or even years in some cases, and you are still responsible for the whole mortgage.

Analyzing an Opportunity So Much That You Miss the Chance to Act on It

Jump in and take a well-researched risk. Sometimes, taking the plunge and diving headfirst into a deal can be the catalyst for realizing your goals. We know that thorough research and preparation are crucial, but there's a delicate balance. Overthinking and excessive planning can lead to missed opportunities. Sometimes, the best lessons come from the experience itself. Embrace the journey, learn along the way, and remember that action is often the key to progress. So, don't be afraid to leap in with confidence and enthusiasm!

Underestimating Your Expenses

Failing to account for all your expenses, including maintenance, taxes, insurance, and property management, can be detrimental. It's essential to create a detailed budget that includes all potential expenses associated with the property. This ensures you have a realistic understanding of your potential cash flow and profitability.

Another thought on expenses is you must have a contingency fund. Having a contingency fund of at least 10% of your budget when renovating real estate projects is like having a safety net in a high-wire act. It provides a crucial buffer against unexpected expenses or unforeseen issues that often arise during renovations. This fund enables you to tackle challenges without dipping into your initial budget or scrambling for additional funds. It brings peace of mind, ensuring that the project can move forward smoothly, even in the face of surprises. With a contingency fund in place, you can navigate renovations with confidence and come out on the other side with a successful, well-executed project.

Overestimating How Much Rent a Property Can Generate

Doing so can lead to financial strain. Be realistic when estimating rental income. Research local rental market trends and compare similar properties to get an accurate idea of what you can realistically charge for rent. The last thing you want is a building that is performing lower than you accounted for.

Overleveraging Yourself by Taking on Too Much Debt

This can be risky, especially if interest rates rise or property values decline. Leverage can be a powerful tool, but it's important not to overextend yourself. Ensure that you have a comfortable cushion to cover debt payments, even in less favorable economic conditions. During 2022 and 2023, when interest rates were rising, many commercial investors saw their monthly mortgage payments skyrocket. Those who were not over-leveraged were able to ride the wave and keep their investment.

Focusing Solely on Property Appreciation Without Considering Cash Flow

This can cause financial instability. Although property appreciation is a nice bonus, it's crucial to have a property that generates positive cash flow. You can be worth millions of dollars in nonliquid property ownership and only have $100 in your bank account. It takes time to sell a property and make it liquid. With a positive cash flow, you have a steady stream of income to cover expenses and build wealth over time.

Forgetting That Location Matters and Emotions Don't

Real estate can have a life-changing impact on your ability to build and maintain wealth. The financial benefits of investing in sound properties in good locations have been tested over time and continually deliver good results. However, those positive outcomes depend on making good decisions before you invest or acquire a property.

This brings us to an investor named Matt who took our Find Fund Flip class. He and his wife, Liz, had recently completed their first flip on a single-family property in a semirural community. Despite their hard work, they barely broke even on the project. Matt wanted to figure out where they had gone wrong.

As Matt shared their experience, our instructor highlighted what they did right. They secured the property well below market value, taking advantage of a unique opportunity after the previous owner's passing. Matt's keen eye for potential led him to the property while exploring a neighborhood he was driving through.

The previous owner had been elderly and had neglected the property for over a year. Matt tracked down the family, who lived on the West Coast, and they were eager to sell without the hassle of making repairs or traveling to the East Coast. Matt and Liz had secured funding from personal sources, including family and friends, which enabled them to move immediately on the house.

The instructor noted that this was a perfect way to find an off-market property as Matt and Liz understood the family's position, needing to sell quickly and easily.

Once the project began, the couple was full of enthusiasm. The property showed great promise with an appealing exterior and spacious interior. However, we have all heard the saying, "location, location, location," and in their eagerness, they overlooked a crucial aspect: location.

The house was right in the middle of the flight path for a busy private charter airport. Living in the middle of a flight path means dealing with regular noise disturbances from planes overhead, which can be pretty frustrating. Also, the house was facing a busy main road. Just like with the flight path, living near a busy road means dealing with a lot of noise. The constant hum of traffic can disrupt peace and quiet, especially if the road is heavily used. Also for families with young children or pets, living near a busy road can be a safety concern.

Ignoring the importance of location became Matt and Liz's first misstep. Although they renovated the property beautifully and it was the perfect fit for a young family, its market value didn't reflect the effort invested. Many potential buyers were deterred by the multiple noise disturbances.

The emotional attachment Matt and Liz developed for their first flip led to their second misstep. They worked tirelessly to add premium finishes and amenities, envisioning a top-tier expensive flip. Despite the neighboring homes not being as luxurious, they priced their property higher than most. Their emotional attachment made them resistant to adjusting the price to align with the market's reality.

As time passed, it was clear their venture wasn't going as planned. The property sat on the market, accumulating holding costs and causing mounting stress. With the guidance of their real estate agent, they eventually dropped the price significantly, barely breaking even.

Reflecting on their experience during the class, Matt recognized the initial oversights. They hadn't thoroughly researched the area to ensure it matched their target demographic.

The biggest mistake, however, was allowing emotions to dictate the level of improvements and the initial listing price. Their attachment led them to include finishes that weren't cost-appropriate for the local market. Holding on to a listing price for too long resulted in substantial holding costs.

With a fresh perspective and a determination to learn from their mistakes, Matt and Liz didn't give up. They approached their next investment more cautiously. The lessons learned from their initial missteps proved invaluable, guiding them toward a successful future in real estate investment.

■ ■ ■

Remember, each point discussed in this chapter is like a building block in your real estate investment journey. Taking them into account will help you build a strong and stable portfolio. Mistakes, as we've emphasized, are not failures but rather stepping-stones toward growth and wisdom. Learning from them is paramount.

The importance of having the right insurance cannot be overstated. Mark's story vividly illustrates how overlooking this crucial step can lead to unforeseen financial setbacks. It's a reminder to all investors to diligently research and secure appropriate coverage for each project.

Equally vital is the caution against taking on too much at once. Our own experiences have taught us the value of focusing on one opportunity at a time, ensuring that each project receives the attention and resources it deserves. This approach can ultimately save both time and money.

The additional tips provided offer valuable insights into avoiding common pitfalls. From conducting thorough due diligence to understanding zoning regulations, each piece of advice serves as a safeguard against potential setbacks. These are the lessons garnered from years of experience, aimed at arming you with the knowledge needed to make informed decisions.

Furthermore, the cautionary tale of Matt and Liz highlights the critical importance of location and the dangers of allowing emotions to dictate investment decisions. Their journey is a powerful reminder to research and objectively assess each potential project.

Ultimately, let our insights serve as an opportunity to embrace the learning process, and let these insights guide you toward a successful and prosperous future in real estate investment.

Chapter 13

Transforming from Investor to Power Player

Eric has been investing for what seems like forever! He is the proud owner of numerous properties, one of which was a mixed-use building with three floors of apartment units sitting atop a trendy ground-floor restaurant. The buildings Eric owns have always been more than just a piece of real estate; they are symbols of his journey as a property owner. But deep down, Eric yearned for more. He didn't just want to breathe new life into old structures; he wanted to create something perfect from scratch. He wanted to become a real estate developer.

Then, fate intervened in an unexpected way. The restaurant at his Main Street property experienced a devastating fire due to improper maintenance of the hood system. No one was hurt, but the building was rendered uninhabitable, and all his tenants were displaced. Eric spent weeks assisting his tenants in finding new homes, negotiating with city officials, and coordinating with engineers on demolishing the ruined structure. It was a challenging time, but Eric managed to navigate through it.

Once the dust settled, Eric found himself standing before an empty lot where his mixed-use building once stood. It was a sight that could have disheartened many, but not Eric. He saw it not as an ending, but as a beginning. He looked at the barren space and envisioned a new building rising from the ashes, a structure that would embody his long-held dream of creating a perfect building from the ground up.

And so, armed with his years of experience working with various developers and his vision, Eric embarked on his new journey.

The transformation from a property owner to a creator was not immediate or even planned, but it was a step that Eric was ready to take. The fire that had seemed like a catastrophe was, in fact, the spark that ignited his path to becoming a true power player in the world of real estate.

Initiating the project was a complex process for Eric. Obtaining initial town approvals, securing funding, and assembling an effective team required considerable time and effort. Recognizing the magnitude of the undertaking, he strategically brought on a partner, Omar, to share the responsibility. Omar not only helped in the day-to-day of the project but also shared in the many decisions that lay ahead and in the excitement of developing.

Later that spring, the project began to materialize as Eric commenced construction on his new 24-unit mixed-use apartment building. His wife, Lina, proposed the name "The Phoenix" for the building—an apt metaphor considering the project's rise from numerous challenges, reminiscent of the mythical bird's rebirth from ashes. This modern luxury building is far from ordinary. It features restaurants, stores, and a rooftop lounge, embodying the resilience, transformation, and grand vision akin to its namesake, the phoenix.

Indeed, The Phoenix was a natural progression for Eric to expand into the realm of real estate development. This new venture was not just a step up; it was an evolution, one that brought a dynamic shift from merely owning properties to essentially giving life to visions from mere sketches on paper to towering structures of brick and mortar. The skills and knowledge that Eric has honed over the years as an investor, such as assessing the profitability of properties, understanding market trends, and forming relationships with other developers, tenants, and city officials, undoubtedly aided him in his journey as a developer. Moreover, his experiences dealing with the unexpected, like the unfortunate fire incident, have infused him with resilience and adaptability, crucial traits for navigating the often unpredictable landscape of development.

For many real estate investors, the move into real estate development can seem like a natural progression. It's an opportunity to take their investment strategies to the next level, increase income potential, and establish themselves as power players within the industry. Real estate development enables investors to be more proactive in their ventures. Instead of merely purchasing existing properties, developers create new ones, dictating the terms of the market rather than just responding to them. This creative control can lead to significant profit margins, far surpassing those in traditional investing.

Becoming a developer also provides an investor with a certain level of prestige and influence. Developers shape skylines, influence urban growth, and contribute to community development. This role can offer a sense of accomplishment and recognition that transcends financial gain.

However, it's essential to note that real estate development is not for everyone. The shift from investor to developer brings with it increased risk and responsibility. Although the potential profits are higher, so, too, are the stakes. Developers must navigate complex zoning laws, manage construction processes, handle larger financing arrangements, and deal with potential project delays or cost overruns. The transition also requires a substantial commitment of time and energy. Development projects often take several years from inception to completion. For those who value the relatively passive nature of traditional investing, this level of involvement might be daunting.

In addition, the barriers to entry are higher in development. This field requires more advanced knowledge and skills, including understanding architectural designs, construction, and project management. Not every investor might be willing or able to acquire these skills.

Although becoming a real estate developer can be a lucrative and rewarding next step for some investors, it's not a decision to be taken lightly. The increased potential for income and influence comes with greater risks, responsibilities, and demands on one's time and skills. Therefore, each investor must carefully weigh these factors before making the leap into real estate development.

What Exactly Is Real Estate Development?

Real estate development, at its core, is a multifaceted business process, encompassing activities that range from the renovation and leasing of existing buildings to the purchase of raw land and the sale of developed land or parcels to others. Real estate development is a big field, and developers are like conductors in an orchestra, bringing all the players together to create a successful property. But, to put it simply, when we talk about real estate development in this chapter, we are talking specifically about starting from scratch by turning a piece of land to one with a usable building on it.

Developers purchase a tract of land, determine the marketing of the property, develop the building program and design, obtain the necessary public approvals, and finance the property development. When the entire process is completed, they then lease, manage, or sell the property. It's a complex venture that requires knowledge across multiple areas, from negotiation and finance to urban planning and construction.

But it's not just about the physical process of transforming land into a building. Each real estate development is, in essence, a journey. It begins with an idea, a vision of what could be. This is where imagination and creativity come into play, envisioning a project that will add value to a community or fill a market gap.

This vision then needs to be translated into a viable plan. This involves meticulous research to understand the market, identify potential hurdles, and determine the financial feasibility of the project. Developers also need to consider regulations, environmental conditions, and community impact at this stage. Following this, the actual construction process begins. This stage requires close coordination with architects, contractors, and various specialists. This stage is about turning the vision into a tangible reality, ensuring that the project is completed on time and within budget. Finally, once construction is completed, the developer needs to focus on attracting tenants or buyers. This involves marketing the property effectively and managing it efficiently to ensure a good return on investment.

Developers like Eric are fascinated by the prospect of executing these various steps and bringing their visions to life. They enjoy the thrill of starting from scratch with a mere plot of land and seeing a building rise up that is entirely their creation. It's not just about the financial returns but also about the satisfaction of contributing to a community, filling a gap in the market, or simply witnessing an idea transform into a physical reality.

Who Should Take the Leap into Development

The number one must-have quality for a real estate developer? It's creativity, hands down! Creativity helps them think outside the box, find clever solutions for tricky problems, stay ahead of ever-changing market trends, come up with one-of-a-kind property ideas that stand out, and figure out innovative ways to market the finished property. Plus, when the going gets tough in the real estate world, creative developers can bounce back and adapt with style.

In the realm of real estate development, creativity is not an optional characteristic—it is a necessity. Much of the success of development projects hinges on the ability to envision possibilities that others might overlook. Developers must be able to look at an undeveloped piece of land or a dilapidated structure and see beyond the current state, imagining what could be.

This creative vision extends beyond the aesthetic aspects of a building, encompassing a comprehension of how space is used and how it interacts with the community and environment. Developers need to predict future trends, anticipate community needs, and find innovative ways to meet those needs while remaining within budget and regulatory constraints.

Creativity also comes into play in solving problems and overcoming challenges that arise during the development process. Each project comes with its own set of challenges, from zoning restrictions to environmental issues to unexpected construction hindrances. It's the developer's task to come up with creative solutions that align with their original vision yet adapt to these challenges. Developers often have to think outside the box to resolve issues related to construction, regulations, and market changes. They must creatively negotiate deals, plan for unforeseen circumstances, and adapt their plans to meet new requirements or opportunities.

Moreover, the design phase of a project is inherently creative. Developers, in collaboration with architects and designers, work on the details of the building, from its layout and exterior appearance to the interior design and amenities offered. They strive to create a unique, functional, and attractive space that stands out in the market.

Last, marketing and selling or renting the property demand creative strategies. Developers must find innovative ways to present their projects and attract potential buyers or tenants.

All in all, the world of real estate development is a canvas for creative expression, where each project represents a unique blend of vision, innovation, and problem-solving. The successful developer is one who can balance melding creativity with practicality to create remarkable properties that serve a purpose and add value to their surroundings.

The Real Estate Development Process

Real estate development is a complex process, encompassing various stages from conception to execution. Each stage demands its own unique expertise and understanding, making the journey both demanding and invigorating. Embarking on a from-scratch project, especially as your first, can be a time-consuming endeavor spanning years. However, every project follows a similar process.

Conceptualization

Conceptualization is the stage in the real estate development process where a developer starts to form a mental image or idea about the potential project. It's the birthplace of an idea, where raw thoughts are transformed into a coherent vision.

In the context of real estate development, conceptualization involves identifying potential opportunities in the market. This could be spotting an underused piece of land in a promising location or recognizing a gap in the market for a certain type of property. For instance, a developer might walk through a declining neighborhood and see beyond the current state of disrepair. They might envision a vibrant community hub, filled with mixed-use buildings that combine residential, commercial, and public spaces.

The conceptualization phase also often involves preliminary research. Developers might look into zoning laws, local real estate trends, demographic data, and potential financing options. They might check the feasibility of their idea at a high level, ensuring there's a realistic chance it could be successful before moving forward. In essence, this is the stage when possibilities are explored and ideas begin to take shape. It's a crucial part of the development process, setting the foundation for all the phases that follow.

Feasibility Study

Next comes the feasibility study. A feasibility study in real estate development is an analysis to determine the viability of a proposed project. This comprehensive assessment includes evaluating market conditions, examining legal and zoning issues, understanding financial implications, and identifying potential risks. It aids developers in making informed decisions about whether to proceed, modify, or abandon a project.

A feasibility study might include the following six sections:

- **Analysis of market demand.** This section outlines the potential demand for your proposed project. For instance, if you're planning to develop a residential apartment complex, you'd need to assess the demand for such housing in the proposed location. You might look at population growth trends, income levels, rental rates, and the rate of occupancy in similar complexes. If there's a shortage of quality apartment living in the area and a growing population, this could indicate strong demand.

- **Competition analysis.** In this section you include an analysis of the competition, which involves studying other similar developments in the vicinity. Sticking with our example, you'd identify other apartment complexes in the area—both existing and planned. You'd look at their occupancy rates, amenities, rental prices, and so on. If there are several new, high-end complexes with low occupancy rates, it may indicate an oversaturated market.

- **Potential return on investment (ROI).** This section describes the potential financial return from your project. You might project rental income based on current market rates, taking into account the cost of construction, maintenance, and other ongoing expenses. Using these figures, you can calculate potential ROI. For instance, if the total development cost is $10 million, and you expect an annual net income of $1 million from rentals, that's a 10% ROI.

- **Risk assessment.** This section identifies potential risks or obstacles and how they would be managed. Risks could include rising construction costs, delays in obtaining permits, changes in zoning laws, or a downturn in the real estate market. For each risk, you'd need a mitigation strategy. For example, you might set aside a contingency budget to cover unexpected cost increases or have a backup plan for marketing the apartments for sale if the rental market takes a downturn.

- **Technical feasibility.** This section of the study looks at whether the project is technically feasible. For example, is the land suitable for construction? Are there any environmental concerns? What about access to utilities and infrastructure?

- **Legal feasibility.** In this section you outline any legal constraints or requirements. These could include zoning regulations, building codes, and permit requirements. You might need to consult with a lawyer or a town planner for this part of the study.

In addition, due diligence plays a large part in conducting a feasibility study. *Due diligence* is a systematic process of gathering and examining information about the property and its broader market context. This rigorous investigation phase uncovers potential problems that could affect the project's success. Consider the scenario of a developer thinking about building a shopping center in a suburban area. The initial feasibility study might indicate a positive outcome. However, during the due diligence process, they might uncover plans for a large mall development nearby. This new information would significantly affect the market analysis, potentially causing the developer to revise their project proposal.

Both a feasibility study and due diligence are critical components of real estate development. They help developers avoid costly oversights and make prudent investment decisions. In the inherently risky domain of real estate, these steps act as essential safeguards.

Acquisition

In the acquisition phase, the developer's goal is to secure the land at a cost that makes the project financially viable. This phase is a pivotal step in the real estate development process that requires a deep understanding of the market, strong negotiation skills, and sometimes even a bit of creativity. It's during this stage when developers either purchase the property outright or secure the rights to develop it. In Eric's case he had the land from the prior building that was destroyed in the fire.

Consider a hypothetical scenario with a developer named John. John identifies an underused property in an up-and-coming neighborhood. He sees potential for a mixed-use development that could cater to the growing population in the area. But first, he needs to acquire the property. John begins by conducting a thorough analysis of the property and its surroundings. He checks the zoning laws, considers the local demand, and calculates the potential costs and revenue. Based on his findings, he determines a price range that he believes would make the project profitable.

Next, John approaches the property owner with an offer. The owner, eager to sell, is open to negotiation. By leveraging his knowledge of the market and understanding of the seller's motivations, John is able to negotiate a price within his target range. With the price agreed on, John finalizes the acquisition, securing the property for his planned development.

The acquisition phase is not just about buying a property, but rather about strategic purchasing. Successful developers, like John in our example, are able to leverage their knowledge and skills to secure properties at favorable prices, thereby laying a solid foundation for their development projects.

Design and Planning

The design and planning stage is a pivotal stage when the developer's vision begins to take shape in a tangible and practical way. In this phase, a team of professionals, including architects, engineers, and urban planners, are brought together. Each has a specific role to play.

Architects are tasked with creating the overall design of the building. They consider various factors such as aesthetics, functionality, and compliance with codes and regulations. Their work includes sketching floor plans, selecting materials, and ensuring alignment with the developer's vision.

Engineers ensure that the architect's design is structurally feasible. They deal with technical aspects like soil weight capacity, HVAC system efficiency, and overall structural integrity.

Urban planners, however, look at the bigger picture. They analyze how the new development will fit into the existing urban landscape. They take into account aspects like traffic flow, pedestrian accessibility, environmental impact, and compliance with local zoning laws.

Throughout this phase, there's a lot of collaboration and problem-solving. Plans are continually refined and adjusted based on input from all team members. The end goal is a detailed, viable plan that's ready for construction. So, in essence, the design and planning stage is a critical step where ideas become blueprints, setting the stage for the physical realization of the development project.

Financing

Securing funding for real estate development is a multistep process and requires careful planning, diligent preparation, and strategic execution. It's not as simple as just walking into a bank and asking for a loan. Developers need to demonstrate the viability of their projects, their ability to manage those projects effectively, and the profitability of their plans.

The first step in securing financing from a bank is conducting the feasibility study we already outlined in this chapter. The feasibility study should include an analysis of the market demand, competition, and potential return on investment. It also needs to consider any potential risks or obstacles and how they would be managed. It helps demonstrate that you've thoroughly researched your proposal and have plans in place to manage any risks.

Once the feasibility study is complete, the next step is to build a development budget and proforma. A development budget and proforma should provide a detailed breakdown of all projected costs associated with the project—including land acquisition, construction, marketing, and operational costs—as well as anticipated revenues. It's also advisable to stress test these numbers under various scenarios to demonstrate the project's resilience in less-than-ideal conditions. In Eric's situation, the land acquisition cost was not a factor as he already owned the property on which he planned to develop. However, his development budget did include a unique cost—the demolition of an existing building on the property.

What Is a Proforma?

In the context of real estate, a *proforma* is a financial statement that projects the future returns on an investment property. It can include potential revenue, estimated operating expenses, and expected cash flow. This helps investors make informed decisions about the profitability of a property before making a purchase.

The proforma is essentially your projected income statement for the project. It includes your anticipated revenues from selling or renting out the property, along with all the associated costs. For instance, if you're developing an apartment complex with 50 units that you plan to rent out at $1,500 per month, your annual gross revenue would be $900,000. Subtracting your estimated annual operating expenses from this figure gives you your net operating income.

Estimating Construction Costs and Marketing Expenses

In your budget planning, construction costs are a critical component. They encompass everything from materials and labor to contractor fees, covering all aspects of the project. Whether it's concrete for the foundation, roofing materials, interior finishes, or landscaping for an apartment complex, these costs are comprehensive.

Ensuring accuracy in construction costs for your budget and proforma involves several key steps. First, examine historical data from similar construction projects to establish a baseline for cost estimates. This includes conducting a thorough analysis of materials, labor, and any other expenses incurred in those projects. Second, consider every facet of the project, not just obvious expenses like materials and labor, in a detailed construction cost estimate. Permits, insurance, and contingency funds for unforeseen costs should also be included. Third, your budget should also take into account nonphysical or soft costs related to the project, such as architectural design fees, engineering studies, permits, legal fees, insurance, and loan interest.

Accurate cost forecasting is essential for successful projects. Without it, there's a risk of going over budget, resulting in financial losses. Using advanced software or professional estimators can aid in precise construction cost forecasting. It's important to note that construction costs can fluctuate. Market conditions can affect material prices, and extended project timelines can lead to increased labor costs. Regular monitoring is crucial to adjust the budget and proforma as needed. Furthermore, estimating construction costs isn't a one-time task. It should occur throughout the pre-development and project design phases to make informed capital budgeting decisions and avoid costly surprises.

In addition to construction costs, marketing expenses come into play after development completion. These include advertising costs, real estate agent commissions, staging expenses for show homes, and more. Once the development is operational, ongoing maintenance costs are factored into the budget. This covers property management fees, maintenance and repairs, utility expenses, property taxes, and insurance.

We understand that this may seem like a lot to handle, but your experience as a real estate investor has well prepared you for the task of assembling this budget. By now, you've likely navigated through the various aspects of budgeting for your investment projects, making this process more manageable and familiar.

Stress Testing Your Budget

Stress testing your budget and proforma is crucial. This involves adjusting your numbers for various scenarios to see how your project would fare under different conditions. Scenarios like a potential rise in construction costs by 10%, rental rates dropping to $1,300 per month, or taking six months longer than expected to fill all the units can help you understand the financial risks of your project. By preparing a detailed development budget and proforma, and stress testing your figures, you can create a solid financial plan for your project, which is essential when seeking financing from banks or other lenders.

Approaching Lenders

When approaching banks for financing, it's crucial to present a well-prepared and thoroughly researched proposal. This includes providing a comprehensive business plan, demonstrating strong project management skills, and having a solid credit history. Banks will also want to see evidence of relevant experience and a track record of successful projects.

Before finalizing the funding agreement, banks typically conduct due diligence to assess the viability and risk of the project. This may involve property inspections, reviewing financial records, and verifying the information provided in the proposal.

It's worth highlighting that while conventional bank loans are a frequently used source of funding, they are far from being the only choice. In fact, smaller local banks, especially those with whom you've built a rapport over your investing journey, can also serve as promising funding sources.

Additionally, other potential financing avenues include syndicated loans and private lenders, not to mention joint venture agreements. Each of these alternatives can offer more appealing terms or increased flexibility compared to traditional loans. However, they also bring their unique considerations and potential risks that need to be carefully assessed. Thus, it's crucial to explore all possible options, including those banks with which you've developed a relationship, to secure the best possible financing for your project.

Securing funding from banks for real estate development is a complex process that requires careful planning, thorough preparation, and a well-presented proposal. Developers need to demonstrate the viability and profitability of their projects, as well as their ability to effectively manage the development process. With the right approach and due diligence, it's possible to secure the necessary financing to bring a real estate development project to life.

Construction

The construction phase is a pivotal point in any development process, transforming the project from mere concept to tangible reality. This multifaceted stage encompasses several crucial responsibilities.

Managing Contractors

Managing contractors is a crucial part of the construction phase, requiring not only hiring but also supervising various professionals who will perform different parts of the construction project. You might need to engage a general contractor to oversee the entire project and specialized contractors for tasks such as plumbing, electrical work, masonry, and carpentry. The management of these contractors can be likened to conducting an orchestra—each player has a unique role, but all must harmonize to create a successful outcome. This involves coordinating their schedules, ensuring they understand and adhere to the project plans, keeping an eye on them during the project, and resolving any disputes or issues that may arise.

For an investor embarking on a ground-up development, finding reliable contractors is a critical first step. There are several strategies you can use to find the right contractors for your project:

- **Conduct an online search.** A simple web search can reveal numerous contractors in your area. Websites like Angi provide listings of contractors along with ratings and reviews from previous clients. Similarly, websites of real estate developers like Ground Up Development can provide leads on potential contractors.

- **Browse social media.** Platforms like Facebook have become increasingly popular for finding contractors. Contractors often advertise their services on these platforms, and you might also find recommendations from other investors in online real estate communities.

- **Ask for referrals.** Word-of-mouth referrals are one of the most reliable ways to find good contractors. Ask other investors, real estate agents, or even friends and family if they know of any reputable contractors.

- **Interview potential contractors.** Once you have a list of potential contractors, it's crucial to interview them to ensure they're a good fit for your project. Ask for references, review their previous work, discuss their understanding of your project, and get a quote for the work. Remember, the cheapest quote isn't always the best—quality, reliability, and a good working relationship are equally important.

- **Check credentials.** Before finalizing a contractor, check their credentials. Make sure they're licensed, insured, and have the necessary permits to carry out the work. There are many websites that provide comprehensive guides on how to find different types of contractors and what to look for.

Monitoring Progress

Another essential aspect is ensuring adherence to plans. This involves vigilant monitoring of the construction process to confirm that the work aligns with the architectural and engineering designs. For example, if a blueprint specifies a certain type of window or a particular wall placement, it's vital that these details get accurately implemented during construction. Regular site visits, contractor meetings, and reviews of the work completed are typical methods used to ensure plan adherence.

Eric and his partner Omar made their constant presence known at The Phoenix site, diligently visiting each day. Their physical presence on the site proved invaluable, helping to prevent myriad potential mistakes that could have otherwise gone unnoticed. Their vigilance and hands-on approach enabled them to spot potential issues before they escalated so they could immediately rectify them. This could range from identifying a minor misalignment in the construction that, if left unchecked, could lead to significant structural problems to noticing a delay in the delivery of essential materials and quickly finding a solution to avoid any downtime.

The proactive and attentive involvement of Eric and Omar at The Phoenix site played a pivotal role in ensuring the smooth execution of the construction project. Their keen eye for detail and daily site visits were an excellent example of effective project management, helping to circumvent potential errors and fostering a successful, efficient work site. Moreover, their daily presence strengthened communication with the construction crew, fostering a collaborative environment where concerns were addressed promptly, and ideas for improvement were openly shared. It also reassured the team that their leaders were fully invested in the project, boosting overall morale and productivity.

Although hiring skilled contractors is a crucial aspect of any construction project, no one understands the intricacies and vision of your project better than you. As the project owner, you have a unique perspective and vested interest that cannot be fully replicated by any contractor, no matter how competent they may be.

Contractors bring their expertise and experience to the table, but you bring the vision, the passion, and the intimate knowledge of what you want to achieve. You are the one who has dreamed about this project, planned it, and put in the hard work to get it off the ground. This personal connection to the project often means you'll spot details others might overlook, and you'll be more motivated to ensure everything goes according to plan.

Adapting to Challenges

Despite meticulous planning, the construction phase often presents unexpected challenges. These can range from unforeseen site conditions like hidden rock formations when excavating, to delays in material delivery, sudden weather changes, or even regulatory amendments. Consider an instance where an unknown underground utility line is discovered during excavation; this might necessitate rerouting or additional permits. The capacity to swiftly adapt and find solutions to such challenges is key to keeping the project on schedule and within budget.

Construction phase extends beyond mere building. It demands active management, thorough attention to detail, and the agility to navigate unforeseen challenges. Each of these elements plays a critical role in ensuring the successful completion of the construction project.

Marketing and Leasing

Marketing and leasing comprise the next-to-last stage of the real estate development process. This state involves attracting tenants or buyers for the development. Marketing and leasing indeed represent a crucial stage in the life cycle of a residential development project. Attracting prospective tenants or buyers for the development is an art that requires strategic planning and execution. However, it is a skill that you will have honed during your time as an investor.

Eric's recent success in running a marketing campaign for a residential development provides a great case study. Leveraging the power of targeted social media ads and local partner outreach, he was able to reach potential renters and effectively communicate the unique selling propositions of the development. Eric used a spectrum of real estate marketing ideas including cold prospecting tactics like email, direct mail, and phone call campaigns, as well as referral marketing. We stress adapting marketing strategies to the digital age where more buyers are turning online to find properties.

A successful marketing campaign for residential development requires a blend of traditional and digital marketing strategies. It involves understanding the target audience, crafting compelling messages, leveraging various channels, and being responsive to market feedback.

Operation

The operation phase is a multifaceted process that encompasses a wide range of responsibilities. It's a crucial stage of the real estate development process when the property manager ensures the development generates an ROI. This involves not only maintaining the property but also managing finances, dealing with legal matters, and fostering good relationships with tenants.

Many developers hand this phase over to a property management company. Although hiring a property management company can be beneficial in terms of handling the day-to-day operations and logistics, there's immense value in the developer staying involved with the property management process.

As a developer, your unique understanding of the property's vision and goals can shape its management and growth. Direct involvement enables you to maintain property quality, understand tenant needs through firsthand interaction, and manage finances effectively. Despite the services of property management companies, a developer's hands-on role is irreplaceable for maintaining the original vision, enhancing property quality, and ensuring sound financial management.

Operations usually involves the following tasks:

- **Maintenance and repairs.** A significant part of property management involves overseeing maintenance tasks to ensure the property remains in excellent condition. This includes regular inspections, scheduling necessary repairs, and preventive maintenance to avoid potential issues. The property's aesthetics, safety, and functionality are paramount to retain current tenants and attract new ones.

- **Tenant management.** A successful property manager knows the importance of maintaining good relationships with tenants. This involves everything from screening potential tenants and handling lease agreements to addressing tenant complaints and conducting move-out inspections. Ensuring tenant satisfaction helps reduce turnover and maintain a steady income stream from rent.

- **Financial management.** Property managers are responsible for managing the financial aspects of the property. This includes setting and collecting rent, managing the property's budget, maintaining financial records, and making sure taxes are paid on time. The goal is to optimize the property's income while minimizing expenses, thus maximizing ROI.

- **Legal compliance.** Property managers must ensure the property complies with all relevant laws and regulations. This includes local housing laws, health and safety standards, and federal laws such as the Fair Housing Act. Noncompliance can result in hefty fines and legal action.

- **Marketing and leasing.** To keep the property occupied, managers must effectively market the property to attract potential tenants. This could involve advertising vacancies, hosting open houses, and working with real estate agents. Once potential tenants show interest, the manager would then handle lease negotiations and signings.

- **Emergency response.** Property managers need to be prepared to respond to emergencies quickly. This could range from natural disasters to power outages or plumbing issues. Having a robust emergency response plan can prevent further damage and ensure the safety of tenants.

- **Sustainability initiatives.** More recently, property managers also take on the role of implementing sustainability initiatives. This could involve energy-efficient upgrades, waste management programs, or water-saving measures. These initiatives not only reduce operational costs but also make the property more attractive to eco-conscious tenants.

Managing a development is a complex task that requires a diverse skill set that you develop while managing investments. It's about maintaining the physical property, managing financials, ensuring legal compliance, and fostering good relationships with tenants. All these tasks contribute to ensuring the property generates a substantial return on investment.

From Investor to Developer: Transferable Skills

It's fascinating how the skills you pick up from real estate investing can give you a leg up when you transition into a developer. It's like going from playing checkers to chess—the basic principles are the same, but there's a whole new level of strategy involved. Just like a surfer riding the waves, as a real estate investor, you learn how to navigate the ebb and flow of the market. You start to spot patterns, get a sense for when things are about to change, and understand what factors can cause a ripple effect. That's an invaluable skill when you're in development because it enables you to anticipate demand, set appropriate prices, and time your projects just right.

Indeed, the concepts discussed in this book are not merely confined to the realm of investing. They are transferable skills that can be applied across a spectrum of endeavors, particularly in the field of development.

Immersion

We understand the importance of immersing oneself in the world of real estate before embarking on any investment. This has enabled us to gain valuable knowledge and insights that have contributed to our success and specifically Eric's success as a developer. You may not think of immersion as a skill. But we have spent a lot of time in this book getting you to immerse yourself in real estate before and during your journey into real estate investing.

Immersion can be an invaluable tool for an investor considering a transition into real estate development. This process of immersion involves fully embedding oneself in the world of real estate development, allowing for a comprehensive understanding of all its aspects. The first benefit of this immersion is a deep and nuanced understanding of the industry. This isn't just about knowing what the final product—the building—looks like. It's about understanding everything from the complexities of zoning laws to the intricacies of construction processes. It's about keeping up with market trends and getting to grips with the various financing options available.

As you immerse yourself in the world of real estate development, you also have the opportunity to build an extensive network within the industry. Spending time in this field will inevitably lead to crossing paths with contractors, architects, engineers, and fellow developers. These connections can become invaluable resources, providing insights, offering advice, and even leading to potential collaborations.

Immersion also allows for hands-on experience. There's a level of understanding that can only come from being directly involved in development projects—whether that involves starting small or observing others at first. This firsthand experience provides a realistic perspective on the challenges and rewards that come with real estate development. Before embarking on The Phoenix, Eric worked with various developers as a real estate broker, learning the ins and outs of their process.

Another critical aspect of development that can be honed through immersion is risk assessment. Development involves higher risks than traditional real estate investing. Becoming adept at identifying, assessing, and managing these risks is crucial.

Although real estate investing and development are related fields, they require different sets of knowledge and skills. The more time spent immersed in the industry, the more these skills can be developed and refined. Immersion is a powerful way to bridge that gap, equipping an investor with the foundation they need to successfully transition into real estate development.

Evaluating Profitability

Another important transferrable skill is found in evaluating the profitability. When you're investing, you're constantly evaluating the potential profitability of properties. You're on the lookout for properties that will give you a good return on your investment. You learn how to look beyond the surface, dig into the details, and make accurate estimates. This skill becomes even more critical in development.

You're not just buying a property; you're creating something new. So, being able to assess the profitability of a project before you even break ground? That's a game-changer.

Relationship Building and Networking

Another skill that seamlessly transfers is the mastery of relationship building and networking that you inevitably acquire. The art of relationship building in real estate investing is like learning a new language. It's all about being able to connect with a wide range of people, from tenants and city officials to other industry insiders. It's not just about making small talk, it's about understanding their needs, their concerns, and working together to find solutions. And when you step into the development arena, those communication skills become even more critical. You're dealing with architects, contractors, local authorities, potential buyers—the list goes on. Your ability to build strong relationships can really make or break a project.

Resilience

Let's not forget about resilience. Investing in real estate isn't always smooth sailing, right? You're going to face unexpected challenges, bumps in the road that throw your plans off course. But here's the thing—each setback is an opportunity to learn, to adapt, and to come back stronger. It's like building a muscle; the more you use it, the stronger it gets. And when you're developing properties, that resilience can be your best ally. Whether it's a delay in construction, a sudden market shift, or a change in regulations, you're ready to roll with the punches and keep moving forward.

Market Awareness

Market awareness, on both macro and micro levels, is another transferable skill. It allows one to recognize trends, anticipate changes, and make informed decisions. For instance, understanding the impact of national economic indicators or recognizing the potential of a burgeoning neighborhood can significantly influence investment and development strategies.

Financing

Financing is another area where knowledge transfer occurs. Understanding various forms of financing, from traditional bank loans to crowdfunding platforms, can help secure the necessary capital for projects. Recognizing one's areas of strength and weakness in this area can enable an individual to seek out advice or partnerships to bolster their financial acumen.

Along the same vein, getting one's finances in order is a skill that applies to both investing and developing. Whether it's maintaining a strong credit score, managing cash flow, or understanding tax implications, these skills are crucial for success in both fields.

Understanding the Types of Real Estate

Understanding different types of real estate, from residential to commercial, is another key skill. Each type has its own unique characteristics and challenges. A multifamily property, for instance, will have different considerations than a retail space.

Working with Partners

Finally, the ability to find and work with partners is a valuable skill. Partnerships can provide additional resources, share risks, and bring diverse perspectives to a project. In investing and developing, strong partnerships can often be the difference between success and failure.

Making the leap from investor to developer might seem like a big step. But remember, you've already got a solid foundation of skills from your investing journey. It's like you've been training for this all along. And with every deal you make, every challenge you overcome, you're building a bridge that takes you one step closer to your goal. So go ahead, take that leap—you've got this!

■ ■ ■

Wow, you've journeyed alongside us through these chapters, witnessing our experiences and insights. Now, it's your time to step onto your own path toward success.

Real estate development isn't just about business; it's a journey. As a real estate investor, you'll hone a unique mix of creativity, sharp analytical thinking, and sheer grit. From the moment you acquire a property, through its development, management, and finally to its sale, each stage has its own set of challenges and rewards. It's like navigating an exciting maze where every turn sharpens your skills.

But before you go charging off into the world of real estate investing, let's recap a bit. Remember, don't get overwhelmed. Yes, the world of real estate can seem vast and complex, but staying organized and focused will be your secret weapon.

Speaking of weapons, don't forget to assemble your dream team. Mentors, partners, contractors—they're all essential players in your real estate journey. Trust us, you don't have to go it alone.

We said it over and over: Education is key. We live in the "golden age of the internet" and it has a vast amount of knowledge for you to absorb. Watch podcasts like ours, *The Real Estate Mix* on YouTube. They are like free master classes just waiting for you to tune in. Soak up that wisdom like a sponge.

When looking at your overall strategy, don't forget value-add investing. Look for those hidden gems, those properties with untapped potential. That's where the magic happens.

Here's a crucial piece of advice: Visualize your future success. If you visualize it, you can own it. And never underestimate the power of discovering what truly drives you. What's your ultimate inspiration? Understanding the purpose behind each business decision will anchor you and keep you motivated, especially during challenging times.

So, fellow future real estate power player, as you close this book and embark on your real estate adventure, remember: Stay organized, seek guidance, educate yourself, leverage value-add opportunities, visualize your success, and never lose sight of your inspiration. With these tools in your arsenal, there's no limit to what you can achieve in the world of real estate investing.

Here's to your success. Go forth and conquer!

Acknowledgments

From Eric Anderson

My journey in real estate has been a whirlwind, starting at a young age with few mentors to guide me. Despite the challenges, I've managed to find success.

That's why I felt compelled to share my experiences in this book—to provide a road map for anyone interested in navigating the real estate landscape.

It all began with the wisdom imparted by my grandparents, who taught me the values of integrity, compassion, and generosity. And the guidance of successful entrepreneurs like my father, Alfred, and Herb, my lifelong business partner.

My journey was further enriched by the love and support of my wife, Lina: her unwavering encouragement and our two wonderful children, Ethan and Emma, have brought boundless joy into my life.

Watching Ethan and Emma grow into exceptional individuals and supporting them in their own paths fills me with pride.

Everything I do in real estate is driven by my commitment to provide a better future for my family. They are my motivation, my inspiration, and my greatest joy.

From Noelle Frieson Friedman

This book and my accomplishments are dedicated to my family, who have shaped me into the person I am today.

To my GranGran, Sheldon, whose dedication to family, community, education, and the power of entrepreneurship as an African

American woman, instilled in me the belief that there are no limits to what I can achieve.

To my mommy, Marenda, who imparted to me faith, vision, and a voice, laying the foundation for all my endeavors.

To my husband, David, my steadfast love, rock, cheerleader, confidant, and partner whose unwavering support is my constant source of comfort, strength, and happiness.

To my son, Brendan, and stepson, Harold, you are the blessings that give meaning to everything I do.

About the Authors

Eric's journey into real estate began at a remarkably young age. At just 22, he took his first step into the world of property investment by teaming up with his father to purchase a single-family home in Montvale, New Jersey. He then went on to purchase a single-family home in River Edge, New Jersey, that was in foreclosure and in need of massive renovations. He renovated with his own hands, increasing the value, and took cash out by refinancing it to buy his first single-tenant commercial building, which he later sold for a substantial sum. This early success provided him with the foundation to forge ahead.

Recognizing the importance of in-depth industry knowledge, Eric pursued his real estate license. Under the guidance of his aunt, an established broker, he learned the intricacies of approaching high-end clients. It was during this time that Eric discovered his preference for commercial real estate. Unlike residential properties, commercial transactions were driven by numbers and logic, devoid of the emotional attachments tied to a home.

In 2011, Eric's entrepreneurial spirit led him to establish the Alexander Anderson Real Estate Group, which swiftly rose to prominence as the foremost commercial and residential real estate brokerage in northern New Jersey. Eric continued to invest in multifamily homes and commercial properties, building a diverse portfolio of rentals. Now, Eric has taken it to another level and is currently in the process of building ground-up developments on the East Coast.

Noelle and Eric first met while Noelle was contracted to market the Hackensack Downtown Special Improvement District, of which Eric was a director. Noelle, a seasoned marketing professional with more than two decades of experience, had honed her skills in revitalizing urban areas, including prominent locales like Manhattan's Lower East Side, and downtown Newark, New Jersey. Her expertise in marketing real estate properties and downtown areas proved invaluable.

In 2018, Eric joined forces with Noelle to fulfill a shared vision. Together, Eric and Noelle recognized a gap in real estate education. They envisioned a school that went beyond passing the mandatory state exam, one that delved into the full spectrum of the real estate industry and its potential for financial freedom. This vision gave birth to the Center for Real Estate Education, a hub that has welcomed more than 15,000 students seeking comprehensive training in pre-licensing, commercial real estate, property management, real estate investing, marketing, and coaching for both agents and investors.

Through their dynamic partnership, Eric and Noelle have not only transformed the real estate landscape but have also empowered thousands with the knowledge and skills to thrive in this dynamic industry. Their collective journey stands as a testament to the impact that passion, knowledge, and a shared vision can have on an entire community.

Index